MW01035397

Open 1
to Our
Fellow Fighters

Written by Rob Phillips and Krissie Lain Garland
Cover created by Chad Leonard, Morgan Phillips
Published by People Matter Ministries

ISBN: 9798484464098
Imprint: Independently published

Dedication

Rob Phillips

For Annie, the strength and love of my life. Your faithfulness has been the greatest example of Christ's faithful love that I could ever experience.

Krissie Lain Garland

Joah and Selah, this project is dedicated to you. You will one day find your place in this complex world. I can only pray that truth will guide you to the God who created you, who loves you unconditionally, who fights for you, and is with you through all of the battles you will face. Let persevering faith help you to understand that we are more than this world. Let love be your light to keep shining forward in the darkness.

Special Thanks

to all of the fellow fighters who contributed to this project, and whose vulnerability may lend strength to others.

Contents

Introduction
to Open Letters

Dear Friends and Fellow Fighters,

When I started this letter we lived in a vastly different time. It feels funny to say that because I have been writing this letter and collecting the included stories for well over a year now, but everything changed in 2020, as you know. For those of us who battle depression and anxiety, it seemed like an unscalable mountain. As is becoming commonplace, in late 2019 and going into 2020, several prominent pastors ended their own lives in despair. This was before the pandemic had even hit the United States. Then the quarantines began, and so many of us who were already in a pitched battle against our own prevailing mental and emotional struggles realized the insurmountable despair that would settle on our nation. In some ways it seemed comforting to me to know that for many, this pandemic would serve as a named enemy to fight. Some whom I had been counseling with for quite a while actually seemed to be better. This was a common enemy to whom we could attribute our struggles. Soon the riots began as well as a very contentious political season (aren't they all?) and despair began to settle on many of our hearts again like a fog moving in from the sea. Opening up normal life again is now the struggle we face even as I finish this letter. I currently live in New York and we were the first state to suffer the pandemic; it seems we will be the last to climb out of it as well. Just last week I woke up at 5AM to a call for help from someone trying to hold on to life and asking why living seems harder than dying. It will only become more difficult in days ahead, and so with urgency I am desperately trying to finish this letter to you, my friends. You who want to exit the fog of despair: the heavy presence of depression and anxiety. There is hope for you, and this hope is found in the One who created you. Yes, we are broken. Yes, our own minds seem to be our worst enemy. No, it wasn't supposed to be this way, but before we can embrace the wholeness that God offers in the Gospel, we must first recognize the depths of our brokenness. So I write to you, my brothers and sisters, as I share the brave and honest accounts of others just like us, others battling every day to stay alive and to reach for thriving. This is our open letter to you. I will begin with my own story, followed by my wife who lived this story with me. Then you will read the story of my friend Krissie who will share the pain of losing her wonderful husband to the battle of depression and anxiety that we are fighting. We will continue with several stories from different people in different places sharing different versions of the same struggles. We will conclude with a message of hope that we trust will give you the encouragement to fight on in this struggle and not give up. These stories are heavy and may perhaps be too dark to read in the midst of your own battle. Some of these stories are unresolved in the personal pain endured by the story tellers. Some of these stories are even a bit graphic and a bit too mature for young readers. We hope you will read them all, but we recognize that some reading this might just need hope and encouragement without more reality. If that is you, my friend, then skip to the last two chapters and drink from the deep well of God's grace and strength. We want you to be encouraged in this battle. I pray you will be blessed. I hope you will see that you are not alone in this struggle. I pray that you will endure. I begin with my own story. This is the first time I am sharing it publicly in full.

Blessings to you my friends,
Pastor Rob

Open Letters to Our Fellow Fighters

The Fog

My lifelong battle with depression and suicidal thoughts

I'll never forget the day the fog finally began to lift because there are some profound things that stick out in my mind. The first thing is that I noticed the sun. It was more than just a moment of appreciating good weather. On that day the sun felt like it was penetrating through my skin into dark corners of my heart that had not seen the light for decades. The second thing that sticks out to me is that my sweet and patient wife looked into my eyes and said "you are back, do you feel better?" It was a random question followed by a sense of victory, without any real discussion. "I do feel better!" I exclaimed. It had been a long and arduous journey to get to this day and I was keenly aware it may not last very long, but it was such a wonderful moment of feeling and recognizing God's tender care for me. Let me start back at the beginning.

Sitting in the back of that old station wagon is a memory I cherish. That old car was like a spaceship for me that brought new worlds to my wondering eyes. My father would load everything up in the back and cover it with blankets. We did not wear seatbelts! My brothers and I would lay across the back and watch the world go by. We would wrestle and fight, and dad would threaten to pull over and leave us somewhere (we knew he was joking) occasionally swerving so that we would knock our heads together and settle down. Nights were the best. We would leave Anaheim and drive over the grape vine (a section of road that went over the Sierra

7

Nevada mountains), entering the high desert and the Joshua Tree forest. I would lie on my back and look out the window at a million stars. It was a trip we made often and it brought nothing but good memories; except for that one time. That one time when there was fog, fog so thick that dad made us put on our seat belts. There was no escaping that fog, and yet, if we sat and waited there would be certain death. I could hear the crunching of metal and see flashing lights. The lights would warn of impending danger and the ominous presence of moving vehicles, but it was always so late and so close. If we sat, we would be hit by another car, maybe even a semi-truck. If we moved forward, we might hit someone else. It was the most unsettling feeling I have ever experienced, and when the fog finally lifted I was able to see what my family had survived with no small wonder.

That fog is the only way I can put into words the struggle I have had with depression and anxiety for over 30 years. This battle began at a young age for me. Before I was a preteen I was already struggling with a constantly recurring thought of suicide. I pictured it daily, sometimes hourly. I would sit in my bedroom alone holding my pocket knife to my wrist and wondering what it would be like. I would practice the movement but would not follow through as the thought of my mom and dad would enter my mind. They would be so sad, and that thought was even more painful than the thought of release.

I needed a release from the fog that had begun the night the babysitter had asked to play a game with me. Mom and Dad were away on a ministry trip. They worked for a youth organization and would often travel to conferences or camps. They did their best to bring us along and Mom usually stayed behind when we could not go, but this time they needed to leave us. I was excited about this babysitter because he was a really cool teen from our youth group at church; an older boy I wanted to be like.

The game was doctor, and there in my parents' bedroom we played the game I try so often to forget. That moment brought shame and the shame lingered like a fog.

In my young adult years the vision of knife to wrist began to change in my imagination, and gun to head became an hourly thought. This darker and still more oppressive thought began in an eerily ironic circumstance. I was engaged to be married and so excited. I was sheltered as a kid and I do not regret it. In spite of being molested as a child, God had spared me from many other types of hurt. Yet, being overly sheltered brings a naïveté. Our family doctor was so trusted. He had saved my mom's life with a diagnosis a few years earlier. When he told my mom that her young adult son (I was only 20 years old at the time) needed a physical before marriage to make sure everything was in order, we believed him. As he examined me he began to make comments about his appreciation for my body. The nurses were dismissed and my mom and fiancé sat in the waiting room. I couldn't believe the doctor game was happening again. He asked me about my sexual history; I had no sexual history. He said he needed to show me how everything worked and asked me to undress. That moment brought more shame and the shame brought more fog. The fog became more oppressive and the knife became a gun.

I struggle to trust men; rightly so. I married a strong woman, a wonderful side effect of my male trust issues. The woman God gave me, my Annie, has been the single greatest blessing of my life. She has endured this fog with me at its thinnest and thickest. I will let her share her part in this story in chapters to follow. I trust her, but she is not a man.

I know Jesus is a man. I trust Jesus. He was abused and He gets it (Hebrews 4:15). Jesus talked about a loving Father who cares for us like a dad loving a prodigal (Luke 15:11-32). This person of the Trinity is described as a man and I struggle to trust Him. I do not have father issues; my dad is wonderful. I have faith issues. I have Heavenly Father issues. My Heavenly Father watched and witnessed, allowed and did not stop both of the times that I was molested. As difficult as it was, I could have handled the sexual abuse. It was the fog that God the Father allowed to roll in during my years of service in ministry that just about ruined our relationship.

I am not exaggerating when I tell you that this part of my story is more painful to talk about than my sexual abuse. I remember the fog of sexual abuse but I *feel* the fog of ministry abuse. I can protect myself from predators but I can not protect myself from seemingly "well-intentioned" people.

Long years of working under insecure leaders felt like decades of abuse. I just wanted to serve God and bless people. All of these insecure bosses were men. All of these men were leaders I initially looked up to and all of these leaders said they only had the best of intentions for me. Four straight abusively "well-intentioned" relationships and 15 years later, I found myself unemployed and unable to sleep. With each new relationship the fog would dissipate for a time only to return more thick than before.

New relationships do not cure previously bad ones, they often just build a quicker gateway to despair. The funny thing about fog is that we adjust. We kind of get used to looking through the cloudiness. It is not until the sun burns the fog away that we realize how difficult it was to move forward and how slow we were actually moving. One night around 3 AM, the Son burned away the fog just long enough for me to see the trouble I was in.

It was a dream that helped me to see and maybe, not ironically, because in that dream I was being attended to by a doctor. Dreams are weird because they defy dimension. In this dream I was on a gurney and both of my wrists were strapped to the side rales. I could see myself, but I was not myself; in some strange way I was observing myself. The "me" I was observing was in obvious torment as I was jerking from side to side, my eyes all black and angry, and I was yelling at the doctor to give me my "release". It took what seemed like ages for a nurse to come in with a needle and as she injected the desired drug into my arm, I saw that it was labeled "bitterness". I woke up and realized that I was in a prison of bitterness. I immediately grabbed my computer and began to write emails of forgiveness. I thought if I offered forgiveness, even without an apology, that maybe I would start to feel better and that my constant fight with depression would soon subside. It was the right thing to do but it did not create the mental and emotional results I so desired. The reason I believe the fog lifted enough for me to see is that it occurred to me that maybe there was not a remedy that would just release me from my struggles. Maybe these struggles were something broken inside of me; and maybe the acceptance that I was broken was the only way for me to learn how to work with and even use my struggles in a productive way. This thought was the beginning of my journey to a healthier place mentally and emotionally.

Open Letters to Our Fellow Fighters

The Stigma

The damaging assumption that all depression is rooted in one's own sin

Growing up in an oppressively religious version of Christianity has done a lot of damage to those of us who struggle with mental illness. One of the most damaging teachings of fundamental conservatism is this: that we possess as believers the ability to lift ourselves out of any struggle with a few verses of Scripture and a personal motivational message. In essence, fundamentalism taught us to become our own saviors and every struggle was deemed to be a faith issue. We sang songs about choosing joy and turning our frown upside down. We wrote books on positivity and produced devotional materials on having the right perspectives.

As a teen who struggled with depression, I would hear pastors and youth camp speakers talk about our attitude being ungodly when we could not find joy. Later on in Bible college I was constantly told I had a spiritual issue because I didn't seem to have the joy of the Lord. Some even questioned my salvation. One individual accused me of not reading my Bible enough. Another individual told me I was spoiled and simply had a weak faith and rebellious heart.

Yes, there was anger in my mind. Yes, there was sadness in my soul. What the preachers and pastors could not see was that I desperately wanted to be rid of my anger and sadness. I had a beautifully real prayer life and I loved reading my Bible. If my faith had been weak as they asserted, I would have been dead years ago from the suicidal thoughts that were so prevalent in my mind. I was still here; I was still fighting the fog.

It is an unhealthy and unwarranted stigma to accuse a depressed believer of being faithless and sinful. The Gospel gives us freedom to be honest about our struggles and to see in them a divine and sovereign work of God's plan and purpose to draw out our struggles and weaknesses so that we can see His victory and strength. I will speak much about the Gospel in this book because it is the only hope for a struggling believer. There is a possibility that someone may have picked up this book who is foreign to the word "Gospel" and its definition. If that someone is you, I would encourage you to stop and and take a moment to read the final chapter of this book so that you can fully understand this word that will be used so often.

It is my opinion and belief through both personal experience and as a result of many counseling sessions I have done with other believers that there are just as many people struggling with depression and anxiety inside the church as there are outside the church; and I believe this all comes down to false assumptions made in ignorance.

It was the stigma that the struggle with depression was simply a struggle with sinful thoughts that kept me from seeking the help I deeply needed for decades. The reality of depression is that it will grow until it is both uncontainable and undeniable. Self-harm is the final result and self-harm is the undeniably exposed result of inward uncontrollable pain.

My own battle with depression became very visible after my second failed pastorate. As I mentioned before, I had been through some abusive relationships during my early ministry years and I needed to take a sabbatical from church ministry. It was during this sabbatical that I developed severe headaches. These headaches were so intense and made me so sick that I would end up being hospitalized for a number of days. After a battery of tests the doctors finally came up with a shocking diagnosis: Post Traumatic Stress Disorder. I laughed at my doctor when he told me and reminded him that I had never served in the military. He began to ask me questions about my past and that conversation began to illuminate for me how much trouble I was in; how much fog I was dealing with in my mind. There were two difficult realities I had to accept that day, two realities that are very negative stigmas for a person called to shepherd God's church:
Reality #1 was that I was a pastor who needed counseling.
Reality #2 was that I was a pastor who needed medication.

A medicated pastor going to see a counselor is the kind of fuel that church gossips build raging fires out of, and I carried this fuel right into my third pastorate. I honestly did not intend to go back into pastoral ministry. What was declared a sabbatical was in reality my hope that I would never return to church ministry, but the Lord in His sovereign grace had other ideas.

In 2012 I agreed to pastor a small church in upstate New York. It was a church in need of love and some leadership to help it become sustainable and culturally effective. I serve at this church still as I am writing this book and have seen God do a wonderful work here these ten years and counting. A number of years ago I lead the church through a big year of necessary change. Any time you change a church that has been around for a while it can bring frustration to the surface. This church happens to be over 225 years old, so there was plenty of frustration ready to boil to the surface. It was during this difficult year that my speech began to slur and I found myself getting dizzy and lethargic. Sometimes I struggled to find every word and this made it difficult to preach. In a moment I will never forget, I sat looking out at a room full of kids while teaching a lesson during Vacation Bible School and suddenly, nothing would come out of my mouth. The words were gone and I stared helplessly at kids and adults with no way of communicating that I was in trouble. I realized in that moment that I could not go on in this way any longer. My depression and anxiety had become so overwhelming that it was now visible. My wife graciously came to my aid as I left the room, went to my office, and laid on the floor for hours wondering if I would ever be okay.

After an honest discussion with my wife and a fellow pastor on our elder team, I finally became honest with the reality that I was broken and in need of help. I had never lived a lie. I had never pretended to be something I was not. I also had never regarded the truth. Up to that moment I had lived as though acknowledging truth was giving in to weakness. I truly believed my battle with depression, anxiety and suicide was the result of feeding the wrong thoughts or not having enough faith. I had been mislead in my understanding of these struggles.

Before I begin to tell you of the incredible work God did in my life as a result of counseling, I must tell you something very important. If you hear nothing else from this book, you need to hear this: *honesty and openness about my struggles saved my life.* I still struggle with depression and probably always will, but in the process of opening up about my struggles, what I thought would be shame and ridicule has been empathy and encouragement. I have met more and more people in the last five years who are fellow strugglers, fellow fighters. Some of these fellow fighters have lent me their courage and strength. Some have modeled prayer in the face of desperate need. Some have given me necessary accountability. Some of my fellow fighters have blessed me with the admission that they have drawn strength for their own struggles because of my honesty. I have found myself in a good company of warriors going to battle every day to spread the hope and joy of the Gospel while walking through a battlefield of mental and emotional struggle. I am so thankful for these fellow fighters whom I would not have known in anonymity.

To all my fellow fighters, I begin this open letter. Take courage; you are not alone in the fog. We are here too; and more importantly, our champion Jesus has left us his Holy Spirit to walk through this fog as a comforting presence. Take strength in His abiding presence, for your fight is no mistake, and it is certainly no surprise. He has a mighty plan to use you just as you are for a Divine purpose; a purpose that will utilize your weaknesses as strengths in a hurting world.

The Freedom to Be Broken

The end goal is not to be fixed, but to see God's glory in the midst of pain

The first time I spoke with a counselor was like lancing a boil that had been filled with infection for far too long. I could not believe all that needed to come out of me. Truthfully, it is still coming out of me, and even as I sit down to write this letter I am experiencing more catharsis as I continue to connect dots and understand even more about my own struggles. As I spoke with my counselor in that first session, towards the end of our conversation I said to him: "I just need you to help me fix what is broken so I can move forward." What my counselor said next comes back to my mind daily, for it offers me freedom that, up to that point, I had never known. Here is what he said: "Rob, the goal here is not to fix you. You are broken for a reason. The goal here is to understand why you are broken and how God can use your brokenness for both your sanctification and for His glory. Going forward, we need to be asking God to use your struggles to accomplish a mighty work."

Those words were cool and refreshing water to a parched and burning soul. Those words put me at ease as they released me from the burden of getting my act together. Those words allowed me to begin to be settled with the idea that what God wanted for me might not be ideal, but that it would be exactly what I needed.

In 2 Corinthians 12 the apostle Paul gives us a glimpse of a very personal struggle.

> (7) So to keep me from becoming conceited
> because of the surpassing greatness of the
> revelations, a thorn was given me in the flesh,
> a messenger of Satan to harass me, to keep
> me from becoming conceited. (8) Three
> times I pleaded with the Lord about this,
> that it should leave me. (9) But he said to me,
> "My grace is sufficient for you, for my power
> is made perfect in weakness." Therefore I
> will boast all the more gladly of my
> weaknesses, so that the power of Christ may
> rest upon me. (10) For the sake of Christ,
> then, I am content with weaknesses, insults,
> hardships, persecutions, and calamities. For
> when I am weak, then I am strong.
> 2 Corinthians 12:7-10 (ESV)

In this passage of scripture Paul is giving an honest assessment of his own life with Christ. Earlier in the chapter he speaks of miraculous and glorious things that God had done in him and through Him. He openly admits there would be a real temptation to boast. Paul then pivots his focus from his glorious moments to the moments of weakness and speaks of a frustrating weakness he calls a "thorn in his flesh". He does not reveal what this struggle is, but whatever it was, it was powerful enough to be attributed to Satan himself. Paul fervently asked for release. Three times he pleaded with God to remove his struggle, and God's divine response was that the struggle must remain. Why would God not remove Paul's struggle? Why would God allow Paul to remain "broken"? Paul's answer is simple: God uses weakness to show His perfect power, and it is a grace when God does so. It is simple to say, but less than simple to appreciate.

By definition, grace is receiving something I did not earn and do not deserve. Paul's weakness was given to him by God's grace. It was a weakness given to him out of unmerited favor. Whether he wanted the struggle or not, it was given to him as something undeserved and unearned.

God has given me the privilege of pastoring a Baptist Church filled with Presbyterians, Lutherans, Pentecostals, Catholics and even former Seventh Day Adventists (even though we meet on Sunday). Each of these people have been teaching me perspectives on worship by how they view and approach God. I would like to think I have been teaching them a thing or two as well! Recently one of our Lutherans gave me a perspective that has helped me with this idea of viewing weakness as a grace. We were having a discussion about trials and I was talking about how the lowest and worst reality in any trial would be death, but that Paul's perspective was "Absence from the body is presence with the Lord". This dear Lutheran sister said to me "Oh Pastor, I can think of a much grander way to process our trial. To think that the same God who created things like solar systems and black holes as well as our own earth and all that is in it would take the time to care about my tiny existence in such a way that he would design a trial specific to the plan and purpose that He wants to accomplish in my life is truly a grace. I'm amazed that He even cares to think of me at all." That is so profound that I could end this letter there, but I will not. It has been an incredible grace to recognize that the all-powerful God of creation wants to reveal his power in and through me by affording me the unmerited favor of being weak and broken. My depression and anxiety need not be seen as a scarlet letter of guilt and shame. My struggle can be seen as a badge bestowed in unmerited honor. I get to enjoy the privilege of watching God take an earthen vessel, cracked and marred, and use it to reveal a treasure that only He can use to show that the excellent power of His glory can only come from him. Paul said it this way:

> (7) But we have this treasure in jars of clay, to show that the surpassing power belongs to God and not to us. (8) We are afflicted in every way, but not crushed; perplexed, but not driven to despair; (9) persecuted, but not forsaken; struck down, but not destroyed; (10) always carrying in the body the death of Jesus, so that the life of Jesus may also be manifested in our bodies. (11) For we who live are always being given over to death for Jesus' sake, so that the life of Jesus also may be manifested in our mortal flesh. (12) So death is at work in us, but life in you.   2 Corinthians 4:7-12 (ESV)

Holiness is Not Happiness

The joy of the Lord is my strength, so why am I so weak?

I grew up at summer camps. This was a perk of growing up in a ministry home. Bug juice, bug bites, bugging my counselors and being bugged by my counselors to get with the program summarizes much of my summer memories. What bugged me the most about summer camp were the weird songs they would make us sing. Now that I am a pastor and a theologian by vocation, I often think back to the words of many of our camp songs and wince with mental anguish at how poor the messaging was in some of these songs. One such song went something like this:

> "The joy of the Lord is my strength, I can't let the Devil steal my joy, because he knows without my joy I would be just a helpless Christian that he could deceive."

This song poses many problems to the understanding of a Christian's health and sanctification. First of all, how is joy defined? If joy is an understanding that God has a plan for my life and therefore can provide hope and purpose, then I do not have a problem with this lyric. If, however, the word joy means having a spirit of happiness, then I, along with many of my fellow believers, am doomed to a life of failure and weakness.

Another song went like this: "Grin again gang and get gung-ho about gladness. Smile sweetly sister so your sins sink sadly away.

25

Buck up brother Bill because a batch of bitter boys becomes a batch of better boys behind a big big smile." Besides being the dumbest lyric ever written (and making everyone who sang it feel awkward), it has a really poor view of our sanctification. Smiling sweetly does not make my sin sink sadly away! The sad reality is that this concept of being sinful because I am not joyful (or happy) is a fallacy that I continue to hear freely dispensed in church culture.

Just yesterday a gentlemen said to me that he felt that depression and anxiety were due to sin. He explained that he himself had been depressed once, but soon after, realized that he was just sinning by not choosing joy. I had to inform him that the definition of clinical depression was not the unwillingness to choose joy, but was rather the *inability to choose joy*, and that to say someone was in sin because they were in depression was tantamount in many cases to saying that a person with cancer was in sin for having cancer.

It is important in this moment to begin to engage theology in the matter of depression linked to sin, and in truth the Bible does link health issues, even mental health issues, to sin. Allow me to explain.

When God created the world, depression did not exist. It is so hard to imagine a world without any emotional or physical pain, but that is exactly the world God created. Adam and Eve were dwelling in a perfect environment with only the experience of joy and tranquility to endure. Enter Adam's sin, and in just a few short moments, there is sadness, guilt, shame, anxiety along with a whole mess of physical ailments rapidly invading that tranquility. It is not soon after Adam's sin that we see both Adam and Eve are very sad and hiding out of fear (Genesis 3). Sad people hiding in fear is a great description for people struggling with depression and anxiety. More bad decisions over the next few generations brought even more heartache. Follow that trend out to today and you have a perpetually broken world in need of repair and restoration. Emotional, or shall I say psychological brokenness, entered this world through the fall just as physical brokenness entered this world through the fall of mankind due to sin.

When someone says to me that they believe depression and anxiety are a result of sin, my next questions and statements are as follows: "When you say depression and anxiety are a result of sin, to what sin are you referring? If you are referring to the original sin of Adam, then I wholeheartedly agree! All depression and anxiety find their root in the original sin of Adam. If, however, you are referring to current sinful behaviors, you may be correct, but you also may be incorrect. Yes, there are times when depression and anxiety are caused by someone's destructive patterns of behavior or sinful decisions. In these cases we must counsel the depressed to change their behaviors and align them to Biblical principles. There are other times, however, when someone is depressed and/or anxious not because they have done anything to cause their struggle, but because either Adam's sin has caused a psychological struggle, or someone else has done sinful harm to the individual being discussed and that individual needs help to heal and recover (the latter is my story).

In stories to follow we will hear about different types of depression and their sources. But in a broad sense, some depression is situational whether self-caused or caused through others, while some depression is psychological. This means that some (if not many) cases of anxiety and depression can happen due to psychological and even physiological problems or situational stresses not resulting from our sinful decisions. Yet, all depression and anxiety ultimately do come from sin, but it is the sin of Adam that resulted in a broken world that has reached down through history and affected us today.

I believe the church has dragged her collective feet when it comes to recognizing that depression and anxiety may not be a result of an individual's sin, but I do not believe it is a new problem. In fact, Jesus dealt with a similar issue in John 9. In this passage the story is told of Jesus healing a man who had been born with physical blindness. Jesus' disciples asked him who had sinned to cause this blindness: the man or his parents? Jesus' response was that the blindness this man was suffering was not a result of either his own sin or the sin of his parents; the blindness, according to Jesus, was given by God so that God's glory might be revealed through him.

Perhaps we need to begin seeing the human condition as more than just a sin issue. Yes, Adam's original sin has caused our broken condition, but in the words of the Apostle Paul, our weaknesses show God to be strong (I Corinthians 1:27-31 and 4:10). Can our weakness, our brokenness, be redeemed for God's glory without being healed? I believe it can and must be redeemable! Again, Paul alludes to his own weaknesses and brokenness in 2 Corinthians 12:8 and states that he had asked God to remove it three different times. He concluded in verses 9-10 that God would allow it to remain to show God's power through his weaknesses.

If it is not already bad enough that Christian counselors, ministry leaders, and pastors are unwilling to consider that some brokenness is allowed by God for His glory, not because of an individual's sin, it is an even deeper tragedy that these same individuals tell those struggling with mental health that it would be wrong to take prescribed medication in order to help properly process information and work through physiological and psychological struggles. The stigma that is placed upon believers using medication to help deal with depression and anxiety (as well as other psychological struggles) is largely from ignorance and often unkindly dismissive to difficulties that persist when dealing with psychological struggles. I am not trying to dismiss the problems of misusing medications or having an unnecessary dependence on them, but we have to begin to acknowledge that some psychological struggles will require medical help in order for the individual to properly receive, understand, and put into practice spiritual principles. Krissie will speak at the end of this letter about some of the issues that must be addressed when it comes to mental health and Cognitive Behavioral Therapy; I would, however, like to give an illustration to help any skeptics reading this book understand why we need to consider the whole person when we talk about psychological struggles such as depression and anxiety.

When I started this letter I was working on an older model MacBook Pro Computer. During the writing process I had to update the RAM in my computer to handle all the updates Mac sent to make my computer ready for the ever-advancing applications (this happens monthly with Mac). My Mac could no longer process information properly, and I would spend hours of wasted time watching the pinwheel of death spin continuously (if you are not a Mac person, it is akin to the blue screen of death a PC gets when it is getting old). As soon as I dealt with the hardware issue, the applications worked much more efficiently. This mildly illustrates the struggle of not addressing the whole person when we are dealing with depression and anxiety. We ministers love to deal with every problem from a spiritual approach, but sometimes the mind needs to be fixed in order to process spiritual truth. This leads me to why I would say we have a theological issue to address in order to truly process how we ought to see our psychological problems.

During my post-graduate studies I had to do a number of research projects on what seemed at the time to be obscure theological topics that I thought would never really amount to much reusable knowledge in my ministry career. One of those topics was the study of dichotomy verses trichotomy. I had no idea how much this study would come back to me during my struggles to understand my own depression later on in life. Both views are viable views of the complete human person and both can offer us an understanding that we need to think more completely in our approach to the complexities of psychological struggles.

We tend to view the human construct in two parts: physical and spiritual. This view of humanity would be called a dichotomous view. Many of the pastors, counselors and ministers I have spoken with see the human construct in this way, therefore when they are dealing with issues of the mind they approach these issues with the idea of dealing with purely spiritual issues. If everything inside of me is composed simply of a spirit, or a soul, or my heart (all these words are used synonymously for most holding the dichotomous view), then the prescription is always the same. It is like the old doctor telling every patient to take two aspirin and call him in the morning. Counselors that have the dichotomous view tend to simply open the Bible and offer a couple of verses that need to be applied with the instruction to go and do it. I realize that I am over-simplifying Biblical counseling, and I am not trying to be demeaning. There are definitely times where applying Scripture is the sole prescription to someone's struggles. But the dichotomous view of the human construct does not allow very much room for there to be other psychological problems taking place that inhibit someone from putting into practice the prescribed truths of Scripture.

What is interesting about the Scriptures is that there is a fair amount of evidence that humans are more than two parts. As someone who sees the human construct in trichotomy, counseling begins to look much less simply as a spiritual prescription and more holistic in approach, especially as it pertains to clinical issues of depression and anxiety. I will explain in more detail why we should see counseling through the view of trichotomy in a few paragraphs, but let me first give a Scriptural support for the trichotomous view.

> (26) Then God said, "Let us make man in our image, after our likeness." (27) So God created man in his own image, in the image of God he created him; male and female he created them. Genesis 1:26-27 (ESV)

As you read through the Bible, there is overwhelming evidence that God is three essences contained in one supernatural being. We call this description the Trinity, and although the word "Trinity" is never used in Scripture, the view that God is three persons is held by most mainline Protestant denominations today. It is the truth of God being the Trinity that helps us see why he states in this verse: "Let us make man in our image…" God is holding a conversation amongst his three persons; it is a dialogue within himself.

Here is the key: if God is going to make man in His own image, and God is three persons, then why would we assume that man is made up of only two parts, instead of three? Surely, if we possess the image of God, then we bear the full image of God, which is in triplicate.

Let me give you another Scripture reference which I believe helps us understand the trichotomy of man.

> (34) But when the Pharisees heard that he had silenced the Sadducees, they gathered together. (35) And one of them, a lawyer, asked him a question to test him. (36) "Teacher, which is the great commandment in the Law?" (37) And He said to him, "You shall love the Lord your God with all your heart and with all your soul and with all your mind. (38) This is the great and first commandment. (39) And a second is like it: You shall love your neighbor as yourself. (40) On these two commandments depend all the Law and the Prophets."
> Matthew 22:34-40 (ESV)

Jesus, quoting the Shema from Deuteronomy 6, was giving an expected answer. This was the passage that the Israelites were to inscribe on their wrists and foreheads, their door posts and fence posts. This passage instructs us to love God in three ways: with our hearts, souls, and minds. Jesus is stating what the law states: we must love God with every part, and there are three parts. This is a trichotomous explanation of the human parts engaged in worship. When one looks at these three words in the greek language (this passage in the New Testament was recorded in the greek language) a picture of God's image begins to emerge.

The word for "heart" used here is the greek word *kardia* and communicates the idea of our physical essence. The word "soul" is the greek word *psyche* and communicates the idea of our animated personhood, or who we identify ourselves as. The word "mind" here is the greek word *dianoia* and communicates the idea of the seat of learning or the part of us that reasons and thinks. This word is used sometimes synonymously with the word "spirit" (although within the english language, we tend to use all three of these words synonymously).

If God is three parts and we are his image bearers, then why is it preposterous to see three parts in the human construct? God the Father is revealed through our human soul. He is to be our very identity. God the Spirit bears witness to our spirit or mind. He is the comforter who communicates the truth of God to us. God the Son took on flesh to save us from our sins committed through the flesh. He received a glorified body after his crucifixion and resurrection, and so shall we receive glorified bodies in our resurrection some day.

So now, let me bring this theology of trichotomy to the counseling realm. When I struggle with depression and anxiety, there is every reason to understand that if my soul is struggling and/or broken, then my soul needs to have help for healing, just as much as my body needs help for healing when it is broken. If my spirit is vexed because of sinful behaviors, then confession is needed along with the application of Scriptural truth. It's not always clear if our mental struggles originate as a spiritual issue or a psychological issue. What should be clear is that not every psychological struggle (from the root word psyche we just learned about) is going to be a spiritual struggle simply requiring a verse and a prayer.

For the sake of the argument, I should take a moment to say that even if I took a dichotomous view of the human construct, I would still very much see the need for dealing with the mind or thinking part of man's spirit in order to help inform physical behavior and response. The scientific knowledge of how neurotransmitters such as dopamine, glutamate and serotonin (as well as others) in our brains affect our ability to think, feel, and reason is increasing rapidly. To think I could regulate these chemicals and the behaviors that result simply through force of mental reasoning is absurd. I could no more mentally convince my gut to let go of fat than I could mentally tell my brain to produce serotonin. There are many things that can affect this process, from proper diet and exercise to genetics to even injury. Even from a dichotomous perspective, I must deal with improper brain function or thought to properly apply spiritual truth. The apostle Paul spoke of this truth in very simple terms: "And do not get drunk with wine, for that is debauchery, but be filled with the Spirit" (Ephesians 5:18 ESV). If the mind is intoxicated, it cannot fully apply truths given from the Holy Spirit to the spirit or mind. The mind must then be sobered to properly receive the truth necessary to inform behavior. The same is true for someone who is not in balance with brain function for reasons other than alcohol, whether these reasons exist due to imbalanced behavioral choices or issues unchosen as a result of genetics or emotional trauma.

In my own life, this was such a freeing truth. When I finally understood that much of my depression was situational, it allowed me the freedom to release myself from the guilt of the struggles I was not causing in my life which in turn allowed me the clarity to see and accept the struggles I *was* causing. As I dealt with what I was directly responsible for, my struggles lessened, allowing me the mental space to begin recovering from the brokenness that was causing other struggles.

I had an open discussion with my doctor one day about seeking more help from medication to bring clarity to my mind. We discussed some options, but elected to wait and see how I did with the counseling I was receiving and the medication I was already prescribed. As I stated earlier, my counselor was clear that the aim of our times together was not to fix what was broken. He wanted to keep as our goal the pursuit of the bigger question of why I was broken and how God could use it for His glory and my good. To the praise of God I did receive healing without more medication. Later on, my doctor was surprised by my clarity and asked what had happened and if I had decided to utilize more or different medication. I told her about what God was doing, and her response was "if that's working for you, keep doing it!" I am praying that she would see the need for Christ in all of this, but my prayer would have been exactly the same if I had chosen the route of more medication.

Not everyone will have my experience. Not everyone will be able to find clarity from the fog without medication. Not everyone will see the fog lift, in spite of their best efforts. The reality is, I myself may be back in the thickness of dark fog again in the future; indeed I anticipate it. This does not mean we have a sin problem, and it does not mean we do not have a sin problem! What it does mean is that God is doing a deep and difficult work of allowing us to see our own weaknesses, our own frailty. He wants us to see this so that we may also see His faithful pursuit and His power to sustain.

I pray that Krissie's part of the letter, and the stories we share will be a balm of hope, encouragement, and empathy to all who read this book. Above all, I pray that you will not give up your fight against depression, anxiety or any other struggle you may have by resorting to self-harm. Seek help, be honest, and surround yourselves with people who care and will listen. They may not understand, and just because they do not understand does not mean they can't love you in your struggle. Give to them the same grace you need from them.

As you continue reading this open letter, I would now like to give you the privilege of hearing from my faithful and precious wife, Annie. You may be reading this book on behalf of someone else and not because you personally struggle with depression or anxiety. I hope her story will be a balm of hope to you as you love your friend or family member through this struggle.

How the Gospel Brings Hope to Anxiety and Depression

His Struggle Became My Struggle

The spouse of the depressed battles the depression, too

It was Easter morning. I remember opening my eyes and trying to sort out where I was. I was in someone else's room, that much was clear as I tried to rouse myself from the dreamy state I was in. There were a lot of mornings like that for me in those early years of my life. I was the daughter of traveling ministers and so many mornings were spent trying to get my brain to take in all the unfamiliar and process where I was. My brothers and I were accustomed to this way of living. We spent every weekday like every other normal American kid in school, but on Friday afternoon we would load up our things and head out for another church, another camp, or another conference with our parents. We honestly did not know any differently and would soon come to appreciate how incredibly special growing up this way really was. Being slammed into the back of a station wagon and eventually a motor home with musical equipment, luggage and all the rest of the stuff that comes with traveling as a family was a normal and welcomed way of life. We would spend fourteen weeks of tour in the summer and every weekend out during the year. I was strangely accustomed to meeting new people, visiting new places, and being with my family most of the time.

So, this particular Easter Sunday morning did not begin as oddly as it may perhaps seem. I climbed out of the bed I was borrowing and stumbled up the stairs to where our host was preparing breakfast. My two brothers were sitting there eating, and before I could notice anything amiss, the hostess took me into her arms and whispered into my ear, "Honey, I don't want you to be frightened but your parents are not here this morning. They had to leave in the middle of the night." I searched her face, but I already knew what had happened. My dear dad had battled for all of my life with a debilitating disease that stole him from us several times a year. At the time, so little was known of how to treat him and he would oftentimes spend the majority of the year in a hospital bed hooked up to tubes and wires and enduring painful surgeries with little to no encouragement that he would ever be healthy again. As a child, I did not know much about his illness and, truth be told, not a lot was known by anyone at that time. All I knew was that when the disease reared its ugly head, our lives inevitably would stop for a while, sometimes a good long while.

The meetings were canceled for that day and plans were made for my grandparents to arrive sometime that evening to collect us. So much felt familiar about this. My dad's disease would often afflict him from out of nowhere, leaving us kids with strangers or family many times for weeks on end. He could be the picture of health one day and headed into emergency surgery the next. We often lived with nagging fear of when it would strike. His disease was a hidden enemy always lurking, threatening to steal our lives. So, we had been here before, and yet I had still had so many questions. I can remember my mom calling a bit later to talk us through what was happening to our dad and to calm our fears and to answer any questions that we might have. The first one I can remember asking her was where we actually were in relation to home. I had blindly followed them here and had not felt an ounce of insecurity about that until I realized that without them there, I didn't even know where I was.

The experiences with my dad and mom taught us to live as pilgrims, sojourners and warriors. Growing up with an ill parent is formative; at least, it certainly was for me. I learned that trusting in God's heart when things are hard and painful is foundational. I learned in those nights where I felt frightened and scared that he was listening to the jumbled and theologically anemic prayers of a little girl who just wanted the safety of a healthy daddy. I learned about commitment to vows made to love in sickness and in health from my mom. I was being discipled in this every day by watching her travel back and forth from the hospital for all those years upon years. She would shuttle us from home to home, and still helped us with homework and middle school drama. I saw her remain joyful in and thankful for the most trivial of things. I saw her sing praises to God in the midst of fear and pain. I saw her cry real, hot tears for the love of her life. I watched her make his hospital room full of color and light and joy. She lived every minute of her life with him. All of it, with all its highs and lows. She lived it *with him.* She was right there for us and right there for him; and I knew it was because of her relationship with Jesus. I understood that her relationship with Jesus gave her the strength to be a warrior.

I did not know it then, but I was marveling at the manifestation of faith in my dad. I visited him once when he was little more than a skeleton at 107 pounds. There was a tube coming out of his nose that was attached to his stomach and when I walked in to see him he welcomed me with a smile that lit up the room. He didn't hide anything from us and we watched him do battle with this disease every day. He walked the path of the Biblical Job with a similar heartbeat: "should we accept only good things from the hand of God and never anything bad?"(Job. 2:9-10). I witnessed him apply 2 Corinthians 1:4 to his life as he used the pain of the trial to minister to countless people around the world with the same comfort God gave to him. He too was a warrior.

I was discipled in the truth about the sovereignty of God in trial. I was discipled in the truth that people that have committed their whole lives to Jesus get sick; and sometimes they even die. I understood that sin brought this suffering, but that God allows pain in our lives and even though we may not understand this, we know from his Word that this is because he loves us and will use pain for our good and for his glory. I learned that God hates what sin has accomplished: broken bodies, broken dreams and shattered lives. I was being discipled about living by faith and trusting God with every-day needs like food and a home. I was being discipled that living this way was really living. I was discipled in the theology of weakness and God's strength.

In those earliest years I felt the weight of limitation. There was nothing anyone could do to remove this from our life. There were days upon days where doctors would run every test, try every new drug, take even more intestine from him and at the end of it all, they would switch off the light in his room with their words ringing in the air, "There's nothing more we can do."

I can not tell you how thankful I am for these informative and foundational years in my life. The Word of God was real. *I knew it.* I trusted it, and as Paul instructs Timothy to continue on in the faith that "first lived in your grandmother Lois and your mother Eunice, and now lives in you also," I know that faith was planted in my heart by the mercy of God and was sown by my parents' faithful example of trust and obedience. *I know it.* It prepared me in ways that I never dreamed. God in His goodness trained me in all of this because in his good plan, he designed my life to walk beside a husband who would battle in another kind of illness. Not an illness of his physical body (although there were many physical ramifications to his illness), but a mental one. God predetermined my life and set me on a path to walk beside a man for life who has deep needs and (praise God for his grace!) I was able to pull from the storehouse of my past the truths I learned as a child; truths of his presence and his goodness in trial. I counted on God's word to be my light and my lamp. I felt the deep peace that comes with his sovereignty and as I felt the weight of my limitations to help my husband, I recalled those formative years and the truths that accompanied them.

In some ways, waking up that Easter morning as a child was easier than what I experienced walking beside my husband through ministry burnout, anxiety, and depression. I say that because I was halfway in with him before I realized that we were on a new path, in a new place, and it took me much longer to wake up and realize that I was in an unfamiliar setting and that I did not know how we got there. He had walked through a diagnosis of PTSD and suffered from a neurological disorder and frightening panic attacks before I even knew what was happening. And when we were "there" , there wasn't a person offering a warm hug; there was no one to reassure me that it was going to be okay and explain what was happening, no one to promise to come and rescue me. I was in a place I did not know, without the knowledge of how I got there, and there was no hope that I would ever leave.

I do not know how to explain the pain of watching someone you love suffer with mental illness; I really don't. It is not unlike watching someone you love waste away in a hospital bed, but it also couldn't be more different. There is something qualifying about physical brokenness. You can see the evidence of something wrong. You see the tubes and wires, you watch them wheeled away in a gurney for surgery, watch their health leave them and sometimes return; but you can *see* it. When someone you love is battling mental illness it is hard to qualify it. When you are in

43

physical pain you can point to a place that hurts and explain it to people and hopefully there is a trained doctor that can tell you what is happening and can prescribe something to heal or aid you. That is not always the case with mental illness.

What I started to notice in my pastor/husband were symptoms. Accompanying the physical ailments, he was tired all of the time, cold in countenance, joyless, short-tempered, and sometimes even displayed a lack of emotion all together. My driven husband had no drive and no desire for life. He was quiet—eerily quiet. I could hardly stomach the quiet. For my part, I honestly didn't know what was going on. I would often ask what was wrong, but he couldn't tell me because he did not understand or explain what it was he was exactly feeling. I did what I knew to do: I kept throwing lots of articles and Bible passages at him. I thought I was helping until I realized that he was shutting me out and avoiding talking to me altogether. At one point he shoved both of his fingers in his ears when I attempted to read him Scripture. I felt panicked! I felt alone and I did not know what to do. Who could I talk to when everyone looked up to him? Everyone needed him to be strong and help them with their problems. I needed him, too! So, I started to manage it all. I had watched my mom manage our house, our ministry, and our lives throughout the years, so it felt natural and normal to do that. I managed our children and the ministry and just kept plodding through. The more I pushed through, the less confident I felt that anything I was doing was helping, and I began to realize that I was losing him in inches.

I do not blame myself for trying to be proactive and in the same sense, I wish so much about those early years had been different. It was the slow admittance that there wasn't a way that I could "fix" this when I began to move from management to dependency. Slowly I admitted that there was not a prescription, or a surgery, or a different set of circumstances that would bring him back to me.

There was no vacation, no mind-awakening speech, nothing that could comfort or exhort him out of the fog. It was as limiting as sitting next to a hospital bed without cures, without comfort and the lights being shut off with the words ringing in your ears, "there is nothing more that we can do." It is a hopeless and limiting feeling and truth be told, I wasn't having it. I could not believe that there was nothing I could do. I cried a lot during this time.

Often times, I am told that it is in retrospect that we learn most of life's lessons. Sometimes, only in hindsight do we realize the hidden hand of God. As I look back on those early years before the diagnosis finally came (which is when the lights all came on for us both!) I am most thankful for the truths of God's Word, the counsel from the Spirit, the righteous record of Jesus, and the example of others as I walked beside the man that I promised to love and to cherish "in sickness and in health". I am thankful for the experiences I had growing up, too. God was my anchor, even when I did not fully understand; I knew I could call upon him for wisdom and strength. He was the warm hug. He was my rescue.

In the years walking next to my husband, I learned that the Holy Spirit is there. He gives light, he reminds me of truth, and he comforts me. He prays for me and he reminds me of the Heavenly Father's promises to me in the loneliest seasons of my life. I learned that Jesus' record means that I did not have to walk through this perfectly because I had his record of long-suffering perfectly as my own. I learned that I can be honest and full of fear and hope at the same time. I learned that God was a better husband, a better Father, a trusted friend and unchanging in his affections for me. I learned that I could give more, die more, laugh more, and cry more honestly than I ever had before; not because of my circumstances but because of the renewing that was happening every day in my life. I learned strength does rise when you wait on the Lord. I learned that it was okay for my kids to bear the burden of their dad's brokenness and that walking beside him in it made their relationship with Jesus beautiful, just like it had for me when I was a child. I learned that I don't have to fix my broken husband, I just need to love him; and I learned that real love does not mean feeling connected and romantic or even unified. I learned that sexual intimacy is not the anchoring hope of a marriage. The anchoring hope of a marriage is Jesus. I learned a covenant is a commitment to *stay* and be quiet even when I need someone to talk to. I learned to be still when I wanted to fight and to cry when I needed to cry. I learned to write in my journal everything I used to say to my best friend/husband and to seek help outside of our marriage without listening to the nagging lie of the enemy that "it will be the end of our marriage if I tell people we are struggling". I learned that the only way through is the daily commitment from Jesus that he will not leave and that he is a stronger, better spouse than I could have ever dreamed of. I learned that God was not making me stronger, but that He was making me die; that he was not making me better, but he was showing me how limiting my sin was to me; and in realizing this, I would experience more of his goodness and grace. I finally understood how to worship.

Currently, my husband is in a season of wellness. Ironically, his diagnosis began while he was working on his doctorate of ministry coursework studying how to counsel the depressed. I remember where I was standing when he came into our room and said, "Babe, I think I have depression." It was a few weeks later that I looked over at night and saw his lips moving as he held a homemade bead necklace one of our daughters had made for him and touched every bead and attached it to a prayer. It was a long journey from there to where we are today. It was years after that when he finally spoke to a counselor, talked to his doctor, and opened up to our church family about his struggles. As I am writing this letter, it has been three years now since the fog began to lift. I believe now that the "not knowing" was the greater burden and that management was a huge detriment. When we knew where we were and we knew how we got there and we weren't afraid to ask for help and direction and prayer, we began to get clarity in the fog. Both of us did.

I know that this is not everyone's story. I have a greater empathy for those who live this difficult reality every day than I ever have before. I can not fathom that pain. I prayed for healing every day when we he was in the darkness. I rejoice in what we have learned but I am glad to no longer be where we were. The complete truth is that walking next to my pastor/husband in this has forever changed me. Much like my father's illness, where there were no guarantees when the illness would strike, always lurking and threatening to steal our lives, I never know when my husband will do battle again and when depression and anxiety will raise its ugly head. When it does, inevitably our life as we know it currently will stop. Without the promise of healing this side of heaven we know that this world can and will bring pain. We are promised that in Scripture. So, as much as I desire for this illness to not get the upper hand, I am not naive to its power, and there are no promises that it will not return. Every trigger sends my heart racing and I have noticed that my hands are starting to shake when I sense something is off with him. I remember so well as a child fearing sleep when my dad was in a season of wellness. I feel it now with my husband in our current season. He still battles daily physical ailments from the effects of this disease. His body is riddled with arthritis and he will stay on a drug for his neurological disorder for the rest of his life; but we do feel more equipped for this journey. We are also promised in Scripture that God will never leave us to walk alone. We are sojourners, pilgrims, and warriors and we won't stop fighting. What I am battling now is *fear*. I fear that I wouldn't survive again. I fear that this next battle would ruin me; that it would ruin *us*. These thoughts sometimes keep me up at night. Where I am resting is that I have a foundational, vertical *hope*. The lowest common denominator in the unknown is Jesus; his faithfulness and his goodness and grace. I can give this part over to the Lord (every day), trusting that the God who brought me to this trial will be faithful to bring me through this trial. There is a quote next to a passage in James in my Bible about not worrying about tomorrow that reads: "You can never see where faith will take you, but you can always see where faith has been". This is the confidence for us: our warrior Jesus has walked this path. He has traveled this path before because he was a pilgrim here, too. He prays. He sees. He knows. He gives us all we need. All to the praise of his grace.

Introduction
of Krissie Garland

As I (Rob) stated before in my story, I grew up in a youth ministry. My parents served in a global youth organization which allowed me to have a lot of friends who were called "staff brats" (the name affectionately given to us by those who had no kids and had all the answers on how to raise kids). Eric Garland and I both grew up in Florida, although he later relocated to New York with his family. We both had a wild streak we thought our parents didn't know about (although I increasingly learn how much moms actually know). We both loved camp. We both wanted to be in ministry. Most importantly to this letter, we both battled clinical depression that most people didn't know about. Indeed, in all of our interactions, Eric and I never once had a conversation about our mutual struggle, as we didn't know we were both battling the same struggles. The topic of depression was taboo in our circles. I continue to survive clinical depression but Eric did not survive. I only had the privilege of meeting Eric's wife Krissie after God took him home. I have found Krissie to be an incredibly strong and wise woman, mom, counselor and widow. As I shared my story with her and the open letter I wanted to write, it was apparent that she needed to be a part of this project. She will be helping to write this letter out of her personal loss to clinical depression as a wife. As a licensed mental health professional, she will also help me conclude this letter with some real and practical wisdom on the importance of understanding clinical depression and anxiety, and the bridges we need to build between Biblical Counseling and brain science. She writes to you now.

His Story, Her Story — Our Story

Telling the story of depression on behalf of those who never got the chance to

As a young girl I dreamed. I danced around the church where my dad pastored as if I hadn't a care in the world. It was my safe place, my home away from home. Never did I see my future and think of a day when life would beat me down, when I would feel hopeless, defenseless, and abandoned. Looking back, I miss that little girl. I miss her dreams. I miss her illuminating smile as she saw the future with such goodness and hope.

This is her story:
It is a story of real life. It is a story of love, of heartache, and of brokenness. It is also a story of forgiveness, second (and third) chances, of hope, of promises, and of redemption.

Growing up as a pastor's kid, I had a good life. I had parents who loved me, a healthy church, and people in the church who cared for me. I was also given every opportunity that a girl could ask for. I was "blessed", to put it into Christian terms. Little did I know that life would be difficult—that the movie I played over in my head would become that of a picture I never knew existed.

Mental health was a topic in our home from a young age. I grew up listening to James Dobson and hearing about his books as my mom followed his work regarding family and mental illness issues. We had an open dialogue within my family about our hurts, hopes, and the day-to-day struggles of life in the ministry. I dealt with depression and anxiety in my own life from time to time. I received counseling for emotional stress caused by my insecurities and feelings of not being good enough, not pretty enough, and not smart enough. Simply stated, I struggled with the feelings of not being "enough." I knew that talking through my thoughts and inner struggles with a counselor helped me. I didn't talk about it much with anyone outside of my counselor and my family. There was a sense of shame attached to seeing a therapist. Pastor's families are not supposed to struggle with these things. My insecurities and depression came and went and were interwoven throughout my formative years, but I found myself back in counseling when I was a senior in high school. I was given the diagnosis of situational depression and was placed on anti-depressants for the first time. They helped significantly while I needed them. However, these topics remained undiscussed outside of our home. I loved the therapist I met with in high school. She taught me so much and her impact continues to be a big part of my life to this day. When I graduated from college, I knew my purpose was to help others. There was not a doubt in my mind because I had experienced what it was like to hurt and what it was like to heal. After doing some missions work in South America, I went to pursue a Master of Arts degree in Marriage and Family Therapy. It was there that I met my fun-loving and charismatic husband, Eric. This is where my story began to shift and become our story together. Our story was a dance between moments of great joy laced with painful times of deep sorrow.

I fell in love with him almost immediately. He had a unique way of connecting with people. His laugh was contagious and his heart was to love others and to point them to a loving God. When I met him I knew that he was special. He loved Jesus and I loved him. We both had big dreams to change the world together. We married in the spring of 2011. We struggled for years to have a child but God in his grace gave us boy/girl twins after 6 years of marriage. They are the brightest lights in our small world. They are, and forever will be, our "abundantly more."

Just over a year later, my husband went home to be with Jesus. He was 31 years old when he took his own life. I still struggle to wrap my mind around how someone who had so much joy, talent, and conviction could also carry so much pain.

My husband had battled deep depression; a depression that he constantly fought, a depression that went unnoticed and ignored, a depression that was shamed and a depression that ultimately took his life. He had carried the weight of it for as long as I knew him. It progressively became worse as he got older and the stressors of life became more difficult. After several doctor visits, Eric was finally diagnosed with clinical depression and ADHD in 2018. He had been tested for several other things, including bipolar, but the test was inconclusive. The psychologist requested we do more testing for bipolar II, yet we never got a chance before he died. We believed that he had it even though he wasn't diagnosed that particular day. We had struggled to find answers as to why my husband's day-to-day thoughts and feelings were not matching up with his spiritual beliefs, his physical symptoms, and his struggles.

My husband wrote about his struggles often. Several days before he died he wrote a note on his phone. I found it days after he had passed away. It reads as follows:

It has been quite a journey for me these last few years. I have hit the lowest of lows. I have battled cancer, addiction, job loss, worthlessness, deep depression, confusion, anger, and hate. There have been days of complete darkness and hopelessness. But there is one thing I will not do… I will not give up.

Yes, I have struggled with what to believe about God. I have had thoughts of "God, you made a mistake on me." But every time (every time) my thoughts go there I am reminded of this picture.

Although I am not active in my addiction, I will always be active in my recovery. The mistakes and sinful choices of my past will be used by God to impact my future. I am thankful that when God looks at me he sees a forgiven, pure man that He created and loves. And while I sometimes lack in my faith, He holds me up and tells me…

"Pick your head up. You are not alone. Don't you ever give up. And when you feel like it is all over. Run to me, and we will walk together."

I am a person of worth because of what Jesus says, not because of what society labels me…

His words serve as an example of what so many people feel and experience daily. He fought hard. He battled his deep wounds of worthlessness and shame. The lies he believed about himself were very powerful. The lies he believed from others often spoke louder than truth. Yet, he continued to fight, to follow, and to love the Lord every step of the way.

We served in ministry together for 8 years. Local church ministry was our heartbeat and it was our "home". Sadly, the ministry is not always the easiest place to be. Ministry can be an extremely lonely and stressful world. My husband never wanted to mess up and he hated to disappoint anyone. He brought in some past wounds and insecurities, but being in the pastorate added a new level to his "need to have everything together". Some of this was placed on him from himself, but some was placed on him from others. His stress became greater as he began to have physical symptoms showing the weight of everything. I saw a big change in him after we lost our little girl before she was born into this world. Soon after that difficult time, my husband was diagnosed with kidney cancer. This was devastating to our family; but what added to the devastation was that we were hit by the shocking fact that Eric was also battling an addiction to opioids. What started as prescriptions for his physical pain became a full blown addiction within a year's time. When we found out about his addiction, he immediately went to rehab and had completely discontinued his use of drugs within another year's time. We are thankful that he stayed clean until he took his final breath. Opioids were an avenue to cover his physical pain for a little while; but sadly, his inner pain continued.

Depression is like a raging river that has a waterfall at the end. It is hard to breathe. It is hard to fight. It is hard to see what is ahead. Though you have moments of relief, it is a struggle to stay above water. That was my husband's last years on earth. He loved God, he loved me, he loved his children, and he loved life; but he could never stop that feeling of drowning; and ultimately he stopped fighting the water and was swept over the edge.

Eric battled clinical depression. Though my husband was fully alive, in some ways I lost him a few years before he passed away. I knew he struggled with depression when I met him. We assumed it was situational; however, it became worse through the years. Although I have a deep knowledge and understanding of depression and mental illness, the picture looked different when it was staring me in the face—when it was walking and breathing right next to me every day. I have the education and experience to help my clients, to relieve them of some of their anguish, to support them in choosing life when they want it all to end. Yet, with that knowledge and experience, I didn't help the man who lay beside me every night. How did I miss it? This thought circles in my mind often. This is the thought, along with guilt, shame, and pain that constantly run through my mind. I am a licensed Professional Counselor. I should have known how to help him. I should have seen this coming. I should have had the answers. I was also his wife. I stood beside a man every day who I could not help completely. I fought alongside of him. I took him to doctors and to counselors. I administered his anti-depressants. I went to AA meetings, Celebrate Recovery, and drove him to rehab. We did life together. I was with him for every step of our journey. However, I missed his last steps that led to his death on that cold winter day.

Mental illness will always be a part of my life. I am not just forced to be in the fight, I am also choosing to be in it. I was called into the mental health field back in 2007. These many years later I have a whole new understanding of mental illness. Christians are not immune to these struggles. It is not something you can wish away or pretend does not affect you. It is an illness. It is as real and painful as my husband's cancer was. Yet, one was cared about and fostered and the other was shamed and ignored; only one of those took his life.

I am praising God that Eric is in Heaven now, free from pain and suffering. We still want him here with us. I wish he could have continued fighting. We miss him every day. Every day I think about the things I could have done differently. I also think about the things that others could have done differently. These thoughts visit me daily. But, I am reminded to think on the things I can do differently today and in the days ahead. I can share his story. I can stand up for truth. I can use his words and his life to help a hurting world understand the effects of depression, anxiety and other mental illnesses. We can use our own stories to help others recognize and provide compassionate understanding to those who fight with their mental health. We can love deeply and genuinely right here and right now.

I now know a life that I did not know before; yet somehow it is okay because I now know a God I didn't completely understand before. I now understand the grace that my goodness did not earn. Living, breathing, God, grace, and the cross have a whole new meaning, and for that I am closer to the Gospel than I ever knew.

My husband wrote this in a journal entry before he passed:

"The truth is, I am not meant to hide. I am meant to live in the freedom the Gospel has given me. I know we all wish we could erase some dark times in our lives. But, all life's experiences bad and good make you who you are. Erasing any of life's experiences would be a great mistake. Mistakes can be our teacher, not our attacker. A mistake is a lesson, not a loss. It is a temporary, necessary detour, but not a dead end.

More than anything I want my brokenness to enlighten those who find themselves in fear, and shame to be able to see His light… To know that Jesus truly is the great Restorer and Redeemer."

So, to my kind, compassionate, outgoing, broken but God-loving husband, this is for you. Let our story, our brokenness, our struggles, our fight and our joys be a light to those who desperately need hope in the darkness. One day, I will dance in the presence of our Maker. But for today, I will run the race set out for me. I will take back the ground that Satan thought he had won, and I will be a voice for the silent.

Introduction
to anonymous letters

The following letters have been written and given to me by individuals that Krissie and I have had the privilege of knowing over the last 5 years. These individuals have all granted us permission to use pieces of their stories in order to help others feel free to be honest with themselves and others. We have kept these stories anonymous, not because the individuals are ashamed of their stories, but because their stories involve other individuals relative to them that may not wish to be connected to this open letter. Certain details you read will have been changed to protect anonymity, but the underlying integrity in the reality of each person's story will remain true.

We have tried to collect and assimilate different letters that describe many, if not most, of the root causes of depression and anxiety. You may find a letter that resonates exactly with your experience, or you may find that your story is told through a combination of these letters. Regardless, our prayer and the prayer of those who have contributed is that you will find encouragement and take courage to keep fighting within these next pages.

As I stated earlier, some of these brave people are still in the process of being honest and getting help. We would encourage the reader to see this collection of open letters as an encouragement to both continue fighting the fight against anxiety and depression, and to be willing to seek help in this fight from others who understand and can help.

Open Letters to Our Fellow Fighters

A Compassionate Fellow Fighter

A letter from someone who wants to help others understand

September houses National Suicide Prevention week. The Center for Disease Control reports that within any two week period, about 8% of Americans experience depression and about 15% of adults will experience depression at some point in their lifetime.[1] Put simply, about one out of every ten people you know struggles with depression.

For most, it is a secret struggle because of the incredibly negative stigma mental illness has in our culture. If a person is diagnosed with cancer, people quickly express their sympathy and support; the patient can almost wear the diagnosis like a badge of honor. However, if a person is diagnosed with a mental illness, others feel awkward around them and keep their distance. The message our society gives is clear: if you have an illness, you have a problem, but if you have a mental illness, you *are* the problem. What's worse is when people verbally ridicule those struggling with depression by either trivializing their suffering (by suggesting they grow thicker

---

[1] Centers for Disease Control and Prevention. (2018, February 13). *Products - DATA Briefs - Number 303 - February 2018*. Centers for Disease Control and Prevention. Retrieved September 26, 2021, from https://www.cdc.gov/nchs/products/databriefs/db303.htm.

skin or man up) or, worse still, they fire verbal arrows at them about how selfish they're being. That is the most unhelpful, counterproductive, uneducated response anyone could give to someone who already feels they don't measure up.

Allow me to step forward and reveal myself as one of those who struggles. I have struggled for years and out of shame, I have kept it from the world. I cannot speak to others' experiences and I dare not set myself up as a representative for those whose battles have been more difficult than my own. I am not a counselor or psychologist; any professional in these fields will easily see that my words here are those of a layman. However, I believe I can speak with authority on what I have experienced and when I look around, it seems others are experiencing the same thing. I will try to offer a glimpse into that world. I do not write as someone who has overcome, but as someone who continues to wrestle with the fog of depression and perhaps because of that, I can more easily relate to those who do the same.

I write now to two audiences: the first are those who do not understand the thought processes of a depressed person. The mind can be a dark place and solitude allows the darkness to grow ever blacker, colder, and more hopeless, and to strengthen its grip around a person's heart. Encourage them, be there for them, let them know how much you value them again and again and again. Leave ridicule at the door, because I promise you that every harsh word will be magnified by the darkness and forged into another harpoon fired right into their heart.

Depression darkens the heart, causing the sufferer to draw ever inward in a silent spiral of self-loathing. Instead of reaching out to others for help, shame robs them of their voice. Believing themselves void of value, shall they forfeit their dignity by exposing their most closely guarded wounds? The shame, embarrassment, and utter humiliation are like iron shackles that lock a person down, ever unyielding and wrestling from them any impulse to break free. And as they lie there in the dark, every mistake they've made, every harsh word told to them, every hate-filled word of contempt and rejection batters their hearts and convinces them that this, *this* is who they really are. That inner voice cries out to them, telling them to deceive themselves no longer and that on its deepest level of brutal honesty, the world would be happier without them. Any fleeting convenience their existence may offer the world is outweighed by obliging others to endure their loathsome presence. The rejection they perceive from others is then adopted by themselves, their hearts convinced they are bankrupt of value. The best they could hope for from others is lip service about how valuable they are with some unconvincing, insincere, superficial clichés told to them not because others believe it's true, but because it's the sort of thing they're expected to say. In this deafening darkness, suicide appears like a key; the final puzzle piece to complete a picture; the answer to a difficult problem on a test; the one thing they can finally do right. The person's own intellect is turned against them. The very concept of someone deeply, honestly, and vehemently wanting them is as tangible as fog; a fairytale so contrary to their experience that it simply cannot be true and most certainly is not meant for them.

My second audience are those who struggle. My dear brother or sister in Christ, you are not alone. As your heart bleeds from the arrows fired at you, know that this present darkness has deceived you with half-truths to make a more convincing lie. Though you and I are more lost than we can imagine, we are also more loved than we have ever dared to dream. You are adored by your maker; the very hairs on your head are numbered (Luke 12:7). Whatever explicit insults or subtle gestures have been fed to you by your fellow creatures aimed at reducing your value, know that your value is derived from your Maker and him alone. Think of those who have cut you down: who are *they* to ridicule you? They are people just like you and their flimsy opinions are like filthy rags next to the divine decree of incredible value given to you by your very Maker who would rather die for you than live without you (John 3:16). Your faults will not negate the love your Maker has for you (Romans 5:8) and the Almighty offers his strength for your weakness (2 Corinthians 12:8-10). I wish I could tell you that people will be kind to you and see you as valuable; that may or may not happen. What *will* happen, what *has already* happened is the unrelenting love of your Maker, whose opinion of you trumps all others, making your value unassailable.

The Suffering Servant

A letter from a pastor who has suffered from many years of ministry service

Serving in Vietnam was a very difficult experience for me. I came back from that war with such brokenness that I struggled to love myself as much as I struggled not to hate what I perceived to be the enemy. God did an amazing work of using all of that turmoil in my life to bring me to salvation, and for that I am thankful. What is amazing about that experience is that, as difficult as it was, it was not as difficult as the pain and struggle that came with serving as a full-time pastor in a large church. I had originally desired to minister in a church with the intention of serving and loving people and seeing them come to Christ and be used for His glory. After decades of serving, I found myself caught between an insecure leader and a needy staff. My final position in the pastorate was serving as an executive pastor (a pastor over other pastors). My final years in the pastorate involved 2 heart attacks and 18 months of PTSD and depression. It is difficult to believe that it was church ministry that caused my PTSD, especially after all that I had experienced in Vietnam.

Insecure leaders suffer with a need for external validation of their performance. In a church this can be particularly difficult because this means looking to people who are supposed to be seeing Christ and asking them to see you. I watched this process play out in a difficult way in the church I served. It all started wonderfully, as

67

God's man passionately preached the Gospel with freshness and excitement. God blessed and our church exploded, but eventually, as all movements do, the excitement began to become less exciting. People started to become critical, and this same man shifted his focus from declaring Christ's glory to protecting his own. As this happened, there was more drive for results by the numbers. To get the numbers, the message became more contextualized to attractiveness in order to compete with the latest trends of growth among other churches. The senior pastor began to focus more and more on his own image and less and less on ministering to the needs of people, not only of the congregation, but also of his own church staff. This is where it became very difficult for me. I found myself caught between a pastor who wanted growth and success above all else, and a staff that could never perform well enough to keep him happy.

One of the most difficult tasks as an executive pastor is to try and cover for what is lacking in the character of an insecure leader, and ultimately this meant I would have to fall on the sword in order that he might be preserved. This meant meetings upon meetings of trying to encourage people without looking disloyal. This meant cleaning up messes I had not made, and filling in gaps I was never meant to fill in. This meant being dumped on by everyone beneath me, and by the insecure leader above me. This meant un-sustainability, and eventually a broken body.

I finally realized remaining in this job would kill me, so I decided to retire early. I gave a year's notice. His response was immediate and hurtful as he uninvited me to staff meetings and proceeded to find ways to give himself permission to no longer have fellowship with me. The friendship I thought we had evaporated into nothing, and the loyalty I had shown was kicked to the curb.

The depression has begun to lift and every day I feel a little better, but it has been a long process of recovery and healing. Through it all, Micah 4:6 has come back to me again and again:

> 6 Not by might, nor by power, but by my
> Spirit, says the LORD of hosts.
> Zechariah 4:6 (ESV)

I thank God for His faithfulness to me during these difficult ministry years and His faithfulness to me now as I continue to recover.

Open Letters to Our Fellow Fighters

Plagued By Fear

A letter from someone suffering severe clinical and chemical depression

I only just survived, and if I'm honest, I continue to just survive. The only difference is that I survive in a better way the longer I live and the more I learn about myself. The day I realized how much trouble I was in was the day I had locked myself in my room with my 2 year old, cowering and curled up in the corner. Thoughts had been running rampant through my head of inflicting pain on someone somewhere with a pen or anything else sharp that I could get my hands on. I could not believe my depression and anxiety had come to this. I was convinced I had gone crazy. When my husband finally came home, I begged him to remove everything sharp from our home.

When I finally told my husband everything, he did what I expected him to do and called the mental health hotline, proceeding to take me to the hospital. He also did something I did not expect: he committed to loving me through my mental weakness. I had waited years to tell him or anyone else anything, convinced they would see me as unfit to be a mother and take my children away from me.

I was in the hospital for two weeks, and came out medicated on Prozac, Seroquel, and Hydroxyzine. They had diagnosed me with severe depression, anxiety and clinical OCD. I was so thankful that

71

the fog was beginning to lift. I was also very angry at my family and friends for a lot of reasons.

Most of my anger was directed at my parents. I had great parents who loved me, but they also had been long-suffering with a family member who had been controlling and abusive towards me. This family member set a precedent of abuse that gave me a weakness for other abusive relationships in high school, and these relationship had caused me to struggle with anxiety with such a severity that I would be paralyzed with trembling and paleness at random times both at school and at home. At 19, these panic attacks began to trigger severe depression and OCD that contributed to escalating suicidal thoughts. The memories of these destructive relationships and the abuse that accompanied them has plagued me throughout my struggle with depression.

For a while in early adulthood I seemed to manage pretty well. I became pregnant and so my boyfriend and I decided to get married. After our first child was born, all of the old thoughts and feelings that haunted me in high school came back with a vengeance. The thoughts of self-harm or harming someone else came back. I was afraid to be left alone. I was afraid of strange things, like baking. Whenever the oven was on, I was convinced I had put my baby in the oven and I would check over and over again to be sure it was just a thought and not a reality. This manic behavior put a lot of strain on my marriage and caused what I thought at the time would be a permanent separation. My parents loved me through that time and cared for me as best they could, but I refused to get help outside of their care. I did not want to be seen as crazy.

Over time, and due to a shared custody agreement, my husband and I reunited and moved back in together. There were many days he would stay home just to help me as I was incapable of dealing with life. We became pregnant a second time, but this time the depression and anxiety finally took its toll resulting in my hospitalization.

The fallout of losing my healthy reputation was worth the safety from the total devastation of harm to myself and to others. But in reality, I lost very few relationships. There were a few who steered clear of my presence and told their interpretation of my story to others. However, for the most part, people not only loved me through my struggle, but they saw me as someone who was honest, trustworthy, and strong. This drew me into closer relationships with those who mattered. These friends, including my husband, have walked through this journey with me in ways I could have never believed before I sought help.

A month after my hospitalization, I found myself sitting in church next to my husband. The pastor, to my amazement, shared with our congregation that he was seeing a counselor for depression and anxiety and needed prayer. I could not believe his boldness and honesty, and I couldn't believe he could share this with his congregation without fear. As we talked later, he shared with me the hard reality that not everyone was receptive and gracious to his honesty, but that those who truly loved him had supported him every step of the way as well. I have found a community in this church family. We share life together, every part of it, the good and the bad and the not so pretty.

For anyone reading this, I want to tell you that those of us struggling with mental illness are regular people working past a disability. Please don't stereotype us. We work hard to overcome our struggles; we just need some extra love and patience. For those struggling behind closed doors, please know that your reputation is not as fragile as you think it is. The people that matter the most will love you through the struggle. Your reputation is not worth the fallout of self-harm. I continue to struggle. You still won't find anything sharper than a plastic butter knife in my home. You can find me on most Sundays (unless it is a really bad one) worshiping alongside other broken and struggling believers, singing songs about my Savior and hearing messages of hope from my pastor.

Abandoned and Just Surviving

A letter from someone suffering the loss of his marriage

My whole body was shaking, my was heart racing, and the room started to spin. I could tell my blood pressure was through the roof and the adrenaline that rushed through my body at that moment made it hard to see. Before I could even understand what was happening, I found myself collapsed on my bedroom floor. My wife of nearly two decades sat across the room with a cold, empty look on her face like I had never seen. It was one of those life-altering moments, a moment where you know that things will never be the same, yet still you have a hard time reconciling all the information coming at you all at once.

I can't say that I was completely surprised by what she had shared with me. I had sensed it was coming, feared it, hoped and prayed against it. Still, as the words poured out of her mouth, I could barely believe them. I had asked her a hard question, one that confronted the distance between us and my growing concern of her fidelity to our marriage. Her simple response, "I don't want to be a pastor's wife anymore" she said, "It's time for you to get a real job". The words stung. With all we had been going through in our marriage the past year I didn't know what this meant. Was she just done with ministry, done with the church, done with Jesus, or done with me? I struggled to get the words out to ask her. "I'm not giving you any guarantees," she replied.

My mind raced through the decades I had known this woman and the many long years of pastoral ministry we had shared. From the first day we had met she had made it clear that her life's intention was to serve the Lord and the church through ministry. She would not even date anyone who did not have the same ambition and desire. Just a few months earlier we had stood together, being commissioned to a brand new path of ministry, pledging together to our church family to be faithful to our calling to plant a brand new church. From that day to this moment I had watched her passion for God fade. She had become distant, hardened, dissatisfied, angry, and critical of church. The irony was not lost on me that after years of ministry, I was thriving in my new role as a lead pastor. Our church was flourishing and our community was strong and growing. I had always loved the churches that I was a part of, but more than ever I felt a sense of belonging in this church and this place. This church, these people, felt like home. At the same time that God was doing amazing things in my life and the life of my church, I watched inexplicably as my wife's spirit died on the vine.

At the same time, I started ministry as a lead pastor, she began working on her own career after a long season of raising our children at home. This was something we had always planned on and I supported and encouraged her to do so. It was her dream job, one that she had worked towards for a long time. At first, I thought her distancing herself from our church and our relationship was just situational as she poured herself into her new role, trying to establish herself in a very demanding career. Her job required a lot of travel, sometimes days and weeks at a time, which meant that on top of my own work and ministry demands, I had greater responsibilities at home than ever before. I was happy to do it. I believed in her and the work she was doing. She is talented and brilliant, and I wanted to see her use her gifts and thrive, to feel the same sense of purpose and calling that I felt in ministry.

As she began to pull away from our church community, I also began noticing changes in her behavior, her values, her long-held beliefs, and even the things that brought her joy that morphed into someone I didn't recognize. This woman who was one of the most spiritually influential people in my life — my counselor, my prayer warrior and spiritual sharpener — lost all interest in the things of God. This woman who would sit with me for hours and talk theology, teach others with me, and come alive in worship and serving others would not even suffer to pray with me let alone discuss the things happening in her heart or our marriage. It was like I was watching my best friend spiritually starve herself into a shadow of what she once was. All the things that brought us together, our shared heart and passion for Jesus and his church were now the things driving us apart.

Once a tireless warrior fighting for the purity and health of our marriage, she had begun crossing boundaries we promised each other we never would cross. Secrecy, private phone calls, changed passwords, late nights or even all-nighters out with other men when she traveled became commonplace. The more concerned and panicked I became, the more I tried to speak into it and call her back, the farther she would run. I saw the secret flirtatious text messages she would try to hide and began catching her in lies on where she was and who she was with. She began changing her appearance, losing weight and secretly spending money (thousands of dollars) on clothes, travel, and beauty products. She opened private bank accounts and secret credit cards racking up piles of debt that I didn't discover until it was too late.

As a pastor for almost two decades, I had seen these red flags before in the marriages of others. I knew what these things suggested; I knew the kind of dangers we faced and where these things can lead to very quickly. Something was feeding her soul and it wasn't me, and it certainly wasn't Jesus. All of these pieces of the puzzle hurled toward me like a locomotive in slow motion. I could see where this train was going, yet still stood powerless on the tracks. Every action, every voiced concern, every plea to get help just made things worse and sent her running faster, farther. Even with all my education, all the theology, all the counseling, all my training and all my years of experience walking with others through this kind of night, I felt helpless to avoid its arrival. I could not help her and she would not let me even if I could.

Now, confronted with questions of unfaithfulness she dropped this bombshell that she was done in ministry and done with the church she once loved and served. I knew in that moment it was a deflection, a way to steer the conversation away from my questions of her fidelity. But the words had been said. Now, she had put me in the place to choose: my ministry or my wife.

Though I loved my church and felt that it was my calling and passion, I would give it up in a heartbeat if it meant I could have her. The terrifying reality was that I wasn't convinced that even if I did leave my ministry it would have any bearing on our marital future. What was happening to us went deeper than that and I knew it. It was those helpless moments where my anxiety and fear reached its crescendo. For the first time in my life I felt completely powerless, helpless, lost and unsure of what to do. It felt like I was alone on the sea in a boat, and the fog had rolled in. I could not tell where the shore began or what direction I was headed. The one person in my life who had been there with me, my constant, my lover, my partner was sailing away. I would call out to her in the fog, but she wouldn't answer. As she sailed away without me, I had one oar in the water and was paddling hard, but only going in circles.

It was the nights alone in the bed we once shared that were the hardest. Endless hours of staring at the ceiling, falling asleep for seconds only to wake in a panic, my heart racing as I realized this nightmare was my new reality. I would pray and beg God to fix it; that he would end this slow marital suicide that was taking place. I prayed that she would consider what this was doing to our marriage, to our kids. I would think of my church family and the people who I loved and what this would mean for them. It was grief, panic, worry, fear, sorrow, compassion, all wrapped into one ceaseless barrage on my soul. In all my restless prayers, night after night, all I heard was silence.

After months of these hard nights, my thoughts, at times, became dark. I never had plans to harm myself. A very close family member had committed suicide years earlier and I had seen the pain that it brought our family. Still, in the depths of those endless nights, I longed for death. Maybe it was sourced in my pride and my desire to not be another pastor whose marriage fell apart. All I know is that death seemed easy compared to the pain and rejection I was walking in. I would pray for it, begging God to end me rather than having to spend a lifetime alone, rather than having to watch my kids go through heartache, rather than having to resign at my church and walk away from the home I loved. I prayed that God would just take me out. I was tired of the unknown, tired of the fear, and tired of the anxiety. I just wanted to go to sleep and not wake up. If God was going to take my wife, take my ministry, take my kids, and take everything I had, why not just let me pass quietly in the night? Hopelessness plagued me. My life felt over. The only word I heard from the Lord in clarity was that this was going to be a hard path, one that he had written for me and one that I would have to walk. He promised to be with me, I believed that and I still do. But if I'm honest, it didn't always feel like he was.

What I did not see at the time was how God was with me, how he kept me and held me. It wasn't always in the way I had hoped he would, but he did. He sent people my way who supported and encouraged me, people along the shore who could see me in the fog and call out the way home, warn me of the rocks and keep me from going deeper into the mist.

I began seeing a therapist to help me navigate and think through what was happening around me. She would listen to my concerns, walk me through my highs and lows and she helped me get on a medication that helped steady my thought process. She also helped me see the reality of things that were hard for me to admit: to name the rejection I was feeling from the one person who knew me best and to grieve the trust I had lost and the relationship I had. She helped me face truths about what was happening that I was not ready to process on my own. Therapy for me was a safe place, a place where I had permission to not be okay or try to put a false spiritual spin on it all.

There were other ways God walked with me and kept me as well. Early on in the breakdown of my marriage I was hesitant to tell the people in my life what was going on. It was not that I was afraid to be vulnerable or transparent, but that I wanted to protect my wife. I was hoping beyond hope that things would turn around. I knew that the more people I involved in what was happening and what I feared was happening, the greater the number of people who would have to be reconciled to my wife if things got better. There was also the fear that in the very act of me trying to get help to save our marriage, I would push her away further. God circumvented my lack of clarity, courage, and action here. The people who knew us, loved us, and walked life with us came to my aid. I can not tell you how many people appeared in unexpected places not knowing what was happening, but being led by the Lord to reach out to me. They had sensed that something was amiss. These were not rubber-necking gawkers or gossips; these were trusted friends; people who loved us both who would bring their sackcloth to sit and grieve with me. These people were my fellow pastors, family, and small group members who saw a need and stepped up and stepped into my mess. I didn't fully grasp it at the time, but these people were God's gift of grace to me as I, the shepherd, became a very needy sheep.

As a pastor, it is easy to fall into a hero complex. If anyone is going to have it together it should be the guy who went to seminary, counsels everyone else, and preaches every Sunday, right? Even if they would never say this, many people in our congregations think this, feel this, believe this. If we are honest, we feed off of that belief; or worse, we believe it ourselves. Our hero complex leads us to act as if somehow our authority and place to lead comes from our own internal super-human source. This can lead us to pride and self-righteousness and leaves us vulnerable to attack. What is most tragic is that it makes the life-giving resource of the body of Christ less able to help us in time of need. It is like we are somehow outside the body system that supplies life and restoration to its wounded parts. It is never easy for me, but the best thing I could do for those I served is admit that as fellow pilgrims in this life, the broken pieces of the fall cut us all. Thankfully, my church had worked long and hard to develop a culture of honesty and transparency, especially amongst its leadership. We regularly walked with each other on this pilgrim path and I felt comfortable and safe unloading my burdens, my weaknesses, and my fears with them.

When I finally shared what was happening with my family, my fellow pastors, and close friends, their response was love, concern, and compassion, not simply for me but also for my wife. They loved her, too. They had seen the marked change in her and what this was doing to us. They grieved for us both, cried for us both, and fought for us both. This small group of people gathered around me. We prayed together, talked together, and cried with one another. There were moments in this chaos, moments I can barely describe that were the most intense times of worship I have ever known. God showed up through them, not in the ways I wanted him to, not in the ways I prayed but in every way I did not know I needed. I was counseled, comforted, rebuked, exhorted and pastored in ways I had never experienced before. It was beautiful! I needed it, especially on those days where every decision felt like life or death and the fog was so thick, I couldn't see my hand in front of my face. I leaned on these people; God was with me and speaking to me through them. They were the voices on the shore I could hear calling me out of the fog.

I found a freedom in this honesty and transparency with these trusted few. We live in a world where we love to post our best days and celebrations on social media. We love to cheer ourselves on for all the beautiful things. It isn't wrong for us to do. We are supposed to celebrate and give God glory in joys and victories. But God gets glory in broken things, too. He has declared that he will. There is something deeply beautiful about this truth. God can get glory in my life even when it is coming apart at the seams. We love the stories of redemption; those stories when God rescues and restores us from all that has been lost and shattered. What we often forget is that there is nothing to be restored that is not first broken, nothing rescued that is not first lost, no wound healed that is not first inflicted. We forget that there is beauty in the waiting that makes our rescue that much more beautiful. This nightmare I found myself in was bigger than me. It was a story that God had written for me. I am God's possession, his servant, and he has the right to lift me up or crush me for his name's sake and his ultimate glory. I couldn't hide it; I had to embrace it as his sovereign plan. Don't get me wrong, I wrestled with God on this path he had taken me on. I wrestled hard. I tried to get out of it. I tried not to follow him through it. I wanted out but he was doing something, and he wasn't playing small.

I wish I could tell you that things got better. I wish I could tell you that there was repentance and restoration and a happily ever after. I wish I could tell you that the hurts stopped, but they didn't. It was a raw and real time where all I could do was lean hard on God and let him use me in my brokenness and weakness.

It happened to be on my birthday: the undeniable evidence came to me that I hoped I would never have to see, the evidence that our marriage had truly been over for some time now. I remember sitting on a porch with my trusted friends as we ugly cried together. We prayed, we mourned, we lamented for what seemed like minutes but was actually more like hours. Those pastors, family members, and friends who had been walking with me encouraged me to get out and to get help. I told my wife and my boys that I needed a few days away to figure things out. The fog had enveloped me and I had no strength left. I needed a few days to meet with my counselors, to get help and figure out what to do next. What happened in those few days amazed me. I gathered together my closest fellow pastors, friends, and family in what could only be described as a council. I told them all how lost I felt, how unsure I was, how I didn't know what steps to take next that would honor God. I submitted myself to the authority of those God had placed in my life. I trusted their clarity in a time when I could not see. I let them carry me when I could not walk. The importance of this cannot be overstated. Not only did these trusted friends give me wise and biblical counsel, but something more happened through these multiple counselors: I began to know that the fog I faced would not be forever. One day the fog would lift and I would look back at that time in retrospect. When the fog lifts, all the fear that you faced while in it seems smaller. All the life and death decisions you made while in it seem easier on the other side. When the fog did lift for me, I was plagued with new concerns, wondering if I had made the right decisions. Walking through this with these other people gave me confidence in those times of reflective doubt because there was not one major decision I made without their voices in it. When those times of doubt came much later, these counselors could speak into it because they were there. They made those decisions with me and sometimes for me. This community brings me so much comfort even after the crisis has passed.

I returned to my family to seek a separation with the purpose of eventual restoration based upon the counsel of these trusted friends. It was clear from the multitude of counselors that I could no longer enable my wife's path away from our marriage and away from our Savior. What awaited me when I arrived back was locked doors, a new alarm system, and a very clear message that I was not welcomed home. She kept my kids from seeing me and had already begun to put a legal action plan into place. She had taken the first steps toward divorce and filed for separation with the intent to dissolve the marriage and be granted primary custody of our children. My deepest fear was playing out before me. What became even more clear, however, was that the fear and anxiety of what could happen was worse than the actual happening, as horrific as it was. I remember the day when the sheriff showed up at our front door with an apologetic look on his face and paperwork to appear before the judge; something happened to me in that moment. God released me from pursuing my wife and gave me a new charge to fight for my kids. In all the anxiety over and pursuit of my wife, my kids had been pushed to the back burner of my heart. Now, released from providing for and protecting my wife and kids, I had a new mission to pursue them. It is hard to describe, but it felt like in just a split second the fog lifted and I knew what I had to do. That day was the last day I felt the crippling fear and fog of my anxiety. God had freed me from it.

Ironically, my circumstances simply got worse from there on out as I spent the next year in and out of court battling for my kids. I had lost everything that was my identity: husband, father, pastor. I was homeless, jobless and living in a friend's basement traveling hundreds of miles each week to spend every second I could with my boys. Still, I was strengthened at just the right moments and felt hope for the future. It's not rational; it does not make sense but that is the best way I can describe it.

I still have bad days, days where anger seeks to destroy me, days where discouragement and disappointment try to steal my joy. Days where I feel deep sorrow and longing for my children when I'm not with them. Days where I wake up alone not really knowing where I am and wondering if this really is my life now. I still question God. He is still silent on why he has allowed all of this to happen. He doesn't owe me an explanation or meaning for what he has allowed. What I see now is the deep work he has undertaken in me through this and that he is *still* working. I have a renewed spirit of compassion for those battling anxiety, depression and other mental struggles. I have a deeper understanding of the body of Christ and my responsibility to not only serve it, but submit to it and be humble enough to be served by it. I have been able to see beauty in the brokenness as the people I once served, cultivated and watered now sustain me with the resources I once gave them. I now worship alongside the people I once led and pastored. They now shepherd me. I know the wounds I have suffered are not fully healed and may never heal on this side of eternity. I know these scars will never go away and that there may be more to come, but I also know that there is beauty in God's redeeming work in them.

At the height of my trial, when my fear and anxiety reached its crescendo, I cried out to God. I wrestled with him and shook my fist at the heavens. It is a moment that will forever be burned into my heart. I was standing at my kitchen sink thinking over all that I had lost and all I feared I might still lose. I questioned God, begging for an answer, calling him out for what felt like abandonment. In that moment he answered me. He didn't answer me in the way I wanted, nor with the specifics of my situation but with the truth about himself. God does that. We seek from him the why and he reminds us of the *Who*. The answers we seek are only found in the depths of his biography. It was a holy moment in the midst of great chaos. I tried to capture it, to put it down in words but they fall short. Still, I want to share this experience with you to hopefully in some small way turn your eyes with me to him...

"God?
Can you hear me?
Are you listening?

God, I have heard of your greatness and wonders. I have read your word and learned of your provision and power. I have listened to the generations before speak of you, sing praise of you and give testimony of your faithfulness. I have believed the unbelievable about your story of redemption and rescue for a humanity you love, pursued and bought back with blood. But I have to be honest with you right now, as if dishonesty is even possible with you.

I don't feel it right now.
I am hurting and the joy I once felt at the sound of your name is getting twisted in the fog of "right now". Where...are....you? Where is the power that I have seen and of which others speak? Where is the protection and provision that you said you would give? It pains me...scares me to even say this blasphemy...but it is where I am. You know it already...right?

I know in your name is the power to move mountains and raise the dead...so why won't you lift me from this place? I know you own the cattle on a thousand hills and the whole earth is yours, so why am I in poverty? I know that yours is the strength and might, so why don't you move a muscle?
Do you still number my tears? Because I've lost count.
Do you still visit the distressed? Because I can't remember the last time I slept through the night.
Are you still the provider of peace and rest? Because I am in turmoil and anguish.
Do you still see the end from the beginning? Because I didn't see this coming.
Do you still heal the sick? Because I am longing for death.

Do you still change hearts? Because mine is weak and hardened and feels heavier by the day.

Do you still heal broken relationships? Because we are shattered.

Do you still break chains? Because this feels like captivity.

Do you still go after missing sheep? Because I feel lost and forgotten.

Are you still the burden bearer? Because I am crushed under this weight.

It is NOT well with my soul! Oh my God. Where are you? Where is this headed?

I hate to even to say these things or feel this way...I feel ashamed at the place I am in.

I feel sorry to even admit it, but my heart is heavy and my flesh is weak.

God help me...help us....I'm bleeding out; crying out.

I am not sure how much longer I can hold out. Are you slipping away or am I?"

His reply came back to my inquisition a true word, if you can even call it language. It was a strong but loving rebuke; soft and gentle, yet thunderous and terrifying. It was a challenging comfort not given in spoken language that one could even write, and not just a feeling. It was an illumination...like a book you have never read but suddenly remember.

"Oh my child, my son, my love. I HEAR YOU. I KNOW. I know this hurt you bear better than you do. I feel it more deeply than you ever have or will. I am not ignorant of this pain...I am feeling it too. I am bearing it with you and for you every moment. I am strengthening you through every breath and every step in ways you can't begin to understand. Don't take my silence for absence! Sometimes my whispering is the only way you can hear me.

You are right. Mine IS the strength and power; the earth melts at the sound of my voice. I could end this hurt with a single word. I could end your poverty with the wind of my breath, but I won't… not yet. You can't cut short my plans for you, for there is no shortcut with the purifying work I am undertaking. You must drink this cup to the dregs because I am preparing you, washing you and remaking you. I am mending the broken pieces, cleansing you of dirt you didn't even know you had. Oh…you have no idea of the beauty I am re-creating here! If there was a better way to accomplish my end, then in my wisdom I would do it…but here we are…where we are. My will be done.

You ask me where this is headed? I've told you; you already know. It's for your good and for my glory, a glory that I have declared that you will share; just don't lose heart in the journey.

Listen to me, my love…my child; these pains WILL turn to joy, not because they will cease to hurt, but because of the beauty they will become. Don't you see the nail-pierced hands?! Can't you feel where the spear went in on that bloody "good Friday"? That day of darkness and death where your sins died, too? These wounds, tokens of death, are now celebrated symbols of life. I turn ashes to beauty, my son…I am The Redeemer of dark things.

I don't just allow these trials…I send them. I give them to you as a gift you don't know how to receive, but trust me…one day…you will. I won't withhold these gifts from you…they are evidence of my love, proof that you are mine.

I DO see the end from the beginning, but for me it is more than just sight; it is experience. I AM everywhere…but what you don't yet understand is that I am also every-WHEN. I AM the end from the beginning. I AM outside of this "right now" you speak of and already there with you as you look back at the journey you would have NEVER chosen, but would NEVER change.

I am there with you already, where the pain and hurt become celebration. Where all your doubting, questioning, and the anguish of your soul will come out of your mouth as songs of praise. It is the most beautiful song you can sing.

I AM already there, where the sorrow will turn to joy and mourning to dancing; not because of the absence of your pain but the presence of my glory. The pain you have felt is real and the scars will not go away, but their meaning will change. No longer will they be reminders of your failures, or your disappointments or the hurts done to you, but they will be trophies of my grace...the marks of your remaking!

My son, my love, my child...your hope in this future will not be put to shame. You will not be disappointed in this remaking that I am working...in fact, your greatest imaginings will not even scratch the surface of the things I have planned for you. I LOVE YOU more deeply than you know and you will spend eternity unraveling the breath-taking mystery of what I am doing in your 'right now'. BE STILL and know that the I AM is with you, for you, and is FAITHFUL to you."

Open Letters to Our Fellow Fighters

My Depression? Rooted in Broken Trust

A letter from someone who suffered abuse from a family member

The acknowledgment of my brokenness happened in a strange way. I was interviewing for a staff position at a youth ministry and one of the interview questions triggered an awareness I had not properly acknowledged as a major source of my mental battles. "Have you ever worked at a youth ministry like this before?" "Yes," was my reply. "Have you worked with children of all ages?" "Yes." The next question is what got me. "Have you ever been sexually abused?" He glanced up at me and said, "Sorry, some of these questions are a little more intense." I responded slowly and quietly: "Yes". It was obvious no one had ever said yes to this question before, and that I might have taken something innocent away from him that day. He struggled through a trained response, asking me if I had ever spoken to anyone about it. "No, you're the first," I responded, trying to hide my embarrassment and frustration at the question. He handed me a pamphlet with a phone number on it. I threw it away in the next garbage can I passed. I didn't take the job.

The reality of my admission gnawed at my thoughts. I decided to pursue some counseling through the college I attended at the time, but I quit after two sessions because the counselor wanted to

95

charge if I continued attending, something she didn't mention until we were halfway through our second session. The truth is, in the short amount of time we met, I attempted to convey my anger at God over the abuse I had endured. She said she could understand how I would be angry at my abuser, but why God? She didn't get it. No one, at least that I have talked to, seems to understand.

About a year later I began dating my future husband. Our relationship had only commenced about two weeks when I began having what I now understand were panic attacks because I was sure he would break up with me when he learned I was "damaged". I had been told as much in my classes at Bible college — "stay away from people who have been sexually involved because they are damaged goods". I struggled to accept his care for me and one day my insecurity bubbled out in tears as I blurted out "my sister, she was…abusive". I wept into his coat as he held me tight and comforted me. I don't remember much of what he said, I just remember that he didn't leave.

I actually struggle with my memory, perhaps because of the way my mind has learned to block things out. I can't recall how old I was when my sister started experimenting on me with her sexual curiosity. I don't know if it was before or after I got my own room, I only know I was younger than 12. My sister would have me role play with her in places like the shower. I believe she was trying to understand adolescents and the struggle of lust without parents who allowed us to ask questions about sex or even puberty, for that matter. I believe she could have chosen differently, but gave into the pulls of sin because narcissism had already taken root. Then one day, after kissing me for a while, she just stopped and said, "This is probably wrong, we shouldn't be doing this". She never touched me again, and never brought it up again. I still wonder (in

total honesty) if an angel entered the room and filled her with
terror or something, because that was the last day it happened. But
I was already wounded, already hurt, and had an unhealthy
understanding of physical affection awakened inside my heart. It
reminds me of Solomon's statement, "Do not awaken love before
its time" (Song of Solomon 8:4).

The remainder of my childhood is a blur, truly, of loneliness,
perfectionism, and crushes that never seemed to relent. I wanted
so badly to know that I could be wanted by a man...that I wasn't a
lesbian.

I once attended a ministry internship in which we spent one
weekend without any communication with other people, except for
some sessions for direction. One of our directives was forgiveness
—to forgive everyone for every sin they had ever committed against
us. I remember at the age of 18, looking up at the big blue sky and
saying "And God, I forgive my sister for all...that stuff she did to
me!" I thought to myself "Okay, that's done. I shouldn't struggle
with it again, because forgiveness is supposed to be absolute."

I now believe only God's forgiveness is absolute. I believe our
forgiveness is much more like a long walk in a circle, with a
backpack, constantly coming back to a thing without realizing it is
still there; then having to shoulder the trauma and bitterness
again, or maybe picking up the burden, examining it and deciding
to set it down again and continue forward, the pain still fresh in
the mind.

As I stated earlier, the man who is now my husband was so faithful
to me in the midst of my brokenness. Early on in our marriage,
some events transpired that brought a lot of the pain of the abuse
to the front of my mind and daily thoughts. A woman I was going

to pursue as a mentor asked me: "Well, have you received your healing?" in response to my honesty about some of the abuse in my past. It was painfully trite, and I avoided her after that. My husband and I have had many conversations about God's goodness and patience with my struggles, even when they turn into sinful attitudes or actions. We come continually back to the question "If God can forgive me of all my sin, can't I in turn forgive my sister?" The answer is not as easy as a simple "yes". Sometimes I don't have the strength not to hate her.

After a few years of studying scripture I did begin to come to the conclusion that there is far too much I now understand to believe in a God who is anything less than sovereign. This theology brought me some comfort, but it also brought me some pain. It can be very painful to recognize and accept that God has, in whatever form, woven this abuse into the tapestry of my life and his will.

What makes this pain so difficult to get over is that while many are eventually able to escape their triggers and abusers, mine is frequently at the most special family and holiday occasions. The pain is like a tide, it may be gone for now but I know it will return eventually.

I tried, for most of my life, to live a deeply good christian life because that is what I thought would prove to God that I loved him. I didn't worry about being "saved" as I hold to the belief that you can't lose a sincere salvation, but I wanted God to know that I did love him in spite of my mental struggles. I had read in the Bible "If you love me, you will obey me" (John 14:15) and so I did my very best. I sought to be everything opposite of my sister. I worked hard to please my parents and never cause them shame by my behavior or choices. But each time I would struggle, the pain would bring questions of, "Where is God in my pursuit towards holiness?!" "Where is his peace and why can't I hear him?!" To this day I still struggle with what "fruit" should look like when you serve a God that has subjected you to, or allowed you to live and relive, evil.

The pain that once plagued my own security in the relationship with my husband now looks like fear for my children. I am terrified that they might suffer abuse at the hands of someone, and that I might not be able to protect them just as my parents had not been able to protect me. That pain has also turned into a pitched battle against depression. I'm ready to entertain the possibility that my depression may not even be tied to my childhood, but I do know that my depressions feels like a persistent longing to be somewhere else, doing something important. I'm constantly plagued by the questions "Why am I here?" and "Why do I matter?" I battle the constant self-induced pressure to be significant, inspirational and important. This is truly my most idolatrous struggle. The pain also looks like not telling very many people about my abuse because they do not know what to do, they do not know what to say, and the most compassionate response is often anguish—they hurt for me and I don't want anyone to hurt. It's why I have never told my parents about my abuse and likely never will. What would it change anyway? It would cause them great grief and bring a rift to our family.

I can hold the hurt so others do not have to, I hold it in to protect others. I believe that one day, I will hand the hurt completely into the hands of the one who took all the hurt to heal me. I have to let go of the expectation that healing will come on this side of glory, or at least, that it will come completely.

A Teen Titan in the Fight

A letter from a teenager offering us eyes to see from a younger perspective

I have struggled with anxiety and depression since middle school, but it was just in the past two to three years that it started to affect my day-to-day life. Being a teenager and struggling with depression and anxiety is a very hard combination. It causes me to miss out on things in life that most teens would consider "normal". It is hard for me to go out alone, drive a car, go to church, and even spend time with my own family. My anxiety stops me from meeting new people and having new experiences and my depression causes me to just stop trying. This way of living can become a habit for any person with mental illness and ends with that person feeling alone, hopeless, and as if there is no way out. Being a teenager and struggling with mental illness adds a whole new layer to the challenges that teenagers face in their journey to adulthood. The emotions that most teens already struggle with are heightened even more when they struggle with anxiety and/or depression.

If you are trying to minister to a teen or young adult who has depression and anxiety, have patience with them. Thank you for asking why we feel the way we do, but please try not to be frustrated when we don't even have a reason or we don't know how to explain it. You may see us as rude or shy, but we are really just fighting a war of anxiety and confusion in our minds that never stops. Don't push us to do things (especially in public) that we aren't comfortable with doing, but instead come beside us and do them with us, taking us by the hand and telling us you are here. If you can see we are "low", don't give us an annoyed gaze or bring attention as to why we are acting "weird" in public, but instead come to us in private and ask how you can help. We don't like to flaunt our struggles or bring attention to them, because we are afraid of being called "emotional, liars, attention seekers, and weak". The worst thing for me is when people push me too far out of my comfort zone in public settings (church youth groups and Christian camps can be the worst for this). This causes major anxiety and an aftermath of depression for the anxiety and embarrassment that I feel.

If you are reading this and you are a teenager who struggles like I do with anxiety and depression, know that God has a reason for your pain. He never causes us pain just to spite us or to teach us a lesson. He has a plan for our struggles and I guarantee it is going to be beautiful.

There are two things I try to remember that help me not to sink too low: the first is to try not to keep my feelings bottled up. I know it is easy to try and "push through them", but you can not do it alone. You need people around you who are going to listen and speak truth to you when you can not tell it to yourself. Don't go by every day saying "I'm fine"; you're not fine and you know it. Find those people who not only comfort you, but who also remind you of the Gospel and the love that Jesus has for you. The second thing that has helped me when I am low or anxious is to accept that this isn't going to change. Thinking to yourself that you need to escape or you need a break from your own mind will lead you down a path that is more difficult to come back from than you know. Instead of wanting your mental illness to go away, lean into it and accept it. God made you perfect in his eyes; accept that truth.

Instead of wishing for it to go away, pick up your Bible and pray for God to help you accept it. You might feel flawed, but you are not, because God doesn't make mistakes. He will help you through the pain. Lean on him for strength.

For those reading this who are struggling or who are in a bad place, know you are not alone. You are never alone. God is by your side every step of the way. He knows the pain that you feel and He hates what the brokenness of this world has done to you. He will fight for you.

Note: The author of this letter wanted to add that she was diagnosed with Thyroid Cancer after writing this letter. This revelation helped her doctors recognize hormone imbalance issues that were the cause of much of her depression and anxiety. The author wanted to communicate how good it was to know the source of her mental struggles and receive medication to help balance her hormones.

From Passion to Burn-Out

A letter from an inner-city ministry leader suffering the effects of ministry fatigue

On a cool and brisk fall morning, I was out in front of our house raking the yard as our two young boys played in the piles of leaves. As I continued my yard work, out of the corner of my eye I noticed a dark silhouette of a man dressed in a cowboy hat and long cowboy trench coat. I did what any protective parent would do and made sure the boys were near me because I wasn't sure what to expect from this unpredictable man. He continued to stumble slowly and every so often, paused and looked over in my direction. Then he stopped right in the front of our driveway, so I felt I had to say something. As a good neighbor I extended a hearty, "Afternoon, how are you?" He said something in a slurred raspy voice that I couldn't quite make out. So I said again, "Afternoon, how are you?" At this point I had made my way to the front of our driveway, keeping myself between him and our boys and could now make out what he was saying: "I'm just a drifter just passing through." I'm not sure what moved me, but a conversation ensued and I learned that this "drifter", ("Cowboy," he called himself), lived in our neighborhood a few streets away and that he was going through some tough times with his wife and family. I could tell from his breath with each slurred word that he was an alcoholic. After what seemed like hours, really only minutes, of our conversation I learned that his family owned farmland where we first lived. As I shared about what I did in youth ministry, he mentioned that he had relatives that were pastors so I knew that he had a bit of a spiritual foundation. Eventually, I would be comfortable enough to drop by his house and continue to check in with "Cowboy" from time to time, offering to help out in any way I could. One time I even traveled three and a half hours away with our youngest son to bring him back to our home to try and help him seek recovery steps, only to see him drift off back into his addiction. At the time I did not realize why God had our paths cross, but eventually, I would see clearly a calling, a call to something for which I was not prepared or equipped.

I am extremely grateful for all God has done in and through the ministry he called us to, yet I know that there are some very critical moments that I chose "suffering for the sake of ministry" and did not pay attention to the harsh impact it was slowly having on me over time. As I stated earlier, we had no idea that what had started as a heart tug several years before with "Cowboy", an alcoholic, would eventually lead us to obey God's calling. After a lot of prayer, seeking counsel, and plenty of tears, we left everything in our wonderful, comfortable, ministry-rich and resource-filled faith culture and co-founded a community outreach center in one of the spiritually darkest and highest welfare areas in the country. This calling would become my everyday ministry to those addicted, overcome with mental illness, displaced, broken, abused, neglected, discarded, and rejected by the culture around them. I didn't feel well-equipped in any way, but I knew and trusted that God, as He says, would "equip the called". God held up his end of the bargain in many mighty ways, blessing me with a pastor's fellowship I could heavily lean on and seek counsel from. I also utilized these men to connect to a few men in our ministry who were in recovery from drugs and alcohol abuse. These men were an answer to prayer that helped launch a successful recovery ministry, impacting and changing many lives. We also had a youth outreach ministry, a weekly Bible study, and did many different community-wide things to serve the greater surrounding community. We even went and visited many churches to share the personal, life-transforming stories and all the other miracles that God was doing in and through our ministry.

Things were going well and God was anointing and blessing what was taking place within the four walls of our ministry center, as well as out in the community. At first, we were not well-received or liked, but eventually we were accepted and well-connected to local group homes and halfway houses and began a volunteer program for many of those men. I was so amazed and thankful for how all of it was taking place within the first three years of the ministry. As bustling and busy as it all was, and as great as things were, I had to take mental note that I was still just one person leading a lot of these things.

At moments, our ministry became unpleasant. There were times when many of the guys I walked the journey of recovery with would relapse, finding themselves in some deep, dark pits. Sometimes I would find myself on call making visits to the local jails and occasionally prison. Other times I would be on the other end of a desperate, life-threatening call just praying that the person on the other end would stay on the phone long enough to not take their own life. We would even have an interruption or two in our recovery group. One time a woman stood up and shouted, "Don't talk about Satan that way, he's my friend". If that wasn't enough to rattle me there were times when our family would receive hateful words and death threats from a mentally disturbed woman (who later would come in and apologize, and also came in many times before to use our shower, drink coffee and have refreshments). All these things would eventually become so commonplace that I wouldn't be taken off guard or surprised with the many different conversations I would end up enduring. What I had not realized was that all of these events, conversations, and situations had started to consume me. I got to the point where I was helping so many people, carrying so many burdens, handling so many desperate situations, that I pretty much put my own needs up on a shelf to make sure everyone else's needs were met. It was as if I was on cruise control with my own life and everything else around me was just happening. This is not to say, however, that throughout this time my spiritual life was crumbling. I believe my relationship with the Lord is what eventually brought me up out of deep despair, depression, and anguish. I am so thankful for rich and anointed times in devotions and times of prayer with God as well as enriching worship at the local church we attended that was so filled with the Holy Spirit. But still, I was only hanging on by a thread.

Ministry life would eventually take a difficult turn, and my wife and I grew tired and weary of feeling alone in the ministry and in desperate need of help. After turning to and pleading with our board, we just knew that there wasn't any help coming any time soon. So I did what I knew, I just kept pushing forward and pouring more of myself into the ministry and into the guys in recovery as well as the youth and maintaining great relationships with the local group homes and halfway houses, residents, staff and directors, hoping that some sort of relief would come.

What I initially thought would be our rescue, became more wear and tear on me and my family. I will avoid sharing the details to protect those involved, but this time in our life nearly destroyed me, my wife, and our marriage. It was truly a time of wooded darkness during which the enemy was relentless and we learned that those who we had considered safe and strong were indeed not safe at all.

We are now a number of years removed from that ministry; a ministry that truly made an impact through a decade of service but also almost devastated my wife, my life, and our marriage. We made the heart-breaking decision to step down from that ministry and out into a new venture. I still grieve the loss of relationships, walking alongside those addicted, overcome with mental illness, displaced, broken, abused, neglected, discarded and rejected by the culture around them, while ministering to those that sought change. Since then, I have gone through a few seasons of rest, healing, and renewal and am now entering a season of redefining my calling as I have joined another ministry where I have been truly blessed to be a part of a spiritually-rich, thriving, and healthy body of servants.

There are several things I learned through this experience and the one that stands out to me the most is the need, when called to a spiritually dark place, to serve with a team of servants. We had an incredible, faithful board, yet never had others to bear up with us in ministry day to day, helping us to shoulder all of the many burdens. Another thing that stood out to me is the need for true transparency and accountability in fellowship. I was a part of a pastor's fellowship and we shared the "surfacey" things we were going through in each of our ministries and basic prayer requests, but never what was "really going on". I had not realized how much I needed healthy community until the damage had already taken place. Lastly, I have learned that the "main ministry" of my wife, my children, and my own spiritual well-being will always need to be attended to and nurtured prior to any one person's urgent, desperate need for help.

My wounds have healed but the scars will always be there and serve as a reminder of God's redemptive work in what could have been a true loss of my marriage and myself. I also hope that my scars will serve to help many others that may be in the midst of their darkest moment, to keep someone from going into that pit of despair, depression, and anxiety, or show those who have gone through something similar that they are not alone; they can reach out and seek counsel as well as help and bear others up. There is nothing too far gone for God to repair, nothing! Even Jesus had scars that he kept as a reminder to show others! As Joseph said in Genesis 50 in response to his brothers' betrayal: "what man intended for the bad, God used for the good!"

Building a Bridge

between Biblical Counseling and mental health

Shortly before my husband took his life, I (Krissie) began to see a problem in our evangelical communities and within our church leadership. This problem was not necessarily new to me, but because it had not directly affected me, I did not take notice as soon as I should have. My husband was suffering. He had prayed and talked with his pastor (in more than one church setting) and to other men in leadership. He had seen doctors; still, he struggled to find understanding as to why he felt the way he did. The church didn't know how to help him except to label his experience as "sinful," as a "lack of faith" or as "consequences to his sin." It is noteworthy to add, that not every church handles these struggles in this way, but it was the truth in our church experiences. If this was the answer to his suffering, then he didn't know what else to do. Was God *that* cruel to punish him for his past or for not being godly enough? I grew up learning that the church was a place for spiritual healing. Yet, I never saw it as a hospital for the sick—the poor, the physically ill, the broken-hearted and those who did not know Jesus (and his healing power through the gospel). It was understood and possibly unintentionally conditioned that if we were spiritually aligned with Christ, then we wouldn't be experiencing illnesses, suffering, or consequences. And mental illness was a problem with the person, not a problem with the brokenness of our world. Carrying this belief only allowed for shame and failure for Christians and lacked understanding and context.

The faulty issue with this belief is that it left no room to help a broken man with a clinical diagnosis and a list of consequences from choices he had made. With my husband's diagnosis and continued struggles, I began to see that many people were falling through the cracks. They were hiding and leaving the faith because they weren't heard or understood. They didn't understand the unconditional love of Christ, because it wasn't being shown to them (whether intentionally or not). These people blamed God, because they couldn't gain his favor enough to be healed. The consequences to this belief ended in loss of hope, in living a life of hiding in shame and, in our personal experience, suicide.

As I've processed this through the years, I realize that I do not have all the knowledge as a ministry leader or as a mental health clinician. I have a heart for helping others find hope through the Holy Spirit and through biblical and clinical interventions. My experiences have brought awareness of the need to educate the Christian community on understanding mental illness and how the church can help their leadership as well as their community be a refuge for the hurting and a place of truth. This chapter will combine both my experience and knowledge as I share and have written it out through my grief journey. After my late husband died, I sat in a closet with tears rolling down my face as I thought to myself, "How can these two worlds connect? How can I help the churches we were a part of understand that they could have handled things differently? How can I help the Christian community understand that issues like mental illness can be valued, seen, understood in both a biblical and clinical way...and that God has given these things as resources to us all?" These two worlds, the Biblical and the clinical, connect through truth and understanding that our Biblical Christian worldview can and does pave a way to allow for biological and scientific truths revealed to us by our Creator. Romans 12:2 tell us this,

"Do not conform to the pattern of this world, but be transformed by the renewing of your mind. Then you will be able to test and approve what God's will is—his good, pleasing and perfect will."

We must not conform to the world, but be transformed by opening our minds to the things that God gives us to provide holistic health. These truths do not violate Scripture or our Christian belief system, but they connect us to his creation.

Foundation

I was raised in a Christian home with a biblical Christian worldview. As shared in my story earlier, I grew up as a pastor's kid and to this day, my parents and my brother serve in local church ministry. When I went to graduate school to pursue a Master's in Marriage and Family Counseling, I knew these things about myself: I loved ministry, discipleship, and listening to the hearts of others. In the first class I attended in graduate school, I sat down in my chair and the first statement my professor made was "counseling is not discipleship." I remember my heart sank as I thought "it's too late to turn back now." That's all I really knew—a Scriptural and spiritual way to help others. My goal in pursuing my education in the mental and behavioral health field was to walk alongside people in their journey towards healing. I quickly realized that I knew very little about brain health and how it affects us in all areas of our lives: mentally, spiritually, emotionally, socially and physically. I began to see that our problems and our sufferings don't always have a spiritual genesis outside of the general sense in which the Fall (sin entering into the world) has affected everything. That is to say, not every problem is a spiritual problem.

I began my journey by searching for and laying my own foundation. Early in my search I read Dr. Ian Jones' book, *The Counsel of Heaven on Earth*. It opened my eyes not only to a Biblical approach, but a clinical approach to counseling. As I read, I began to see the intricate ways God made us and the impact sin had on us—not only spiritually, but physically. This book was most helpful as I studied to find solid answers to link the two together—Biblical truth and clinical interventions. The bridge from Biblical and Scripturally-based counseling to the clinical side of therapy needs to be built and it needs to be both biologically and spiritually solid. Many in the Christian world are led to feel as if they are wrong if they look outside of Scripture to find answers when it comes to mental illness. This statement needs to be read loud and clear: Scripture is God's inerrant Word. Everything in it is true. It is without error. It holds every answer we need to live. Scripture teaches us that God created each individual person as unique. He knit us together (Psalm 139: 13-14). He didn't just throw us together. God created every detail to make us who we are. He created us, body, soul, and spirit. To ignore the majestic way he did so can only limit us as we acknowledge the fullness of his sovereignty. He created our brains in such a way that we will most likely never fully understand the full capacity or complexity of their functioning. He gives people intelligence, resources, and skills to help us find ways to heal sickness and prevent diseases. Once we understand this connection, we begin to build a necessary bridge to comprehensively help others and ourselves. When Adam and Eve disobeyed God and hid from him, God asked them, "where are you?" He asked this question not because he didn't know where they were, what they had done, or what they were experiencing, but because he wanted them to acknowledge it and confess their standing to Him. God knows all things and is at work in and through all things. He wanted them to think and use their cognitive and emotional capacities to see their actions and understand the consequences, thus leading to a lifetime of needing God's guidance and a community with others. Throughout the Old Testament, God established the need for community, a group of people with resources and abilities to help one another thrive and survive in a world ravaged by sin and suffering. The New Testament church would become the ultimate expression of God-given community. But God also offered us the will to choose to acknowledge our need for help and to utilize the resources he has provided to give us that support. Acknowledging our sufferings, mistakes, and sins doesn't take away our brokenness or our pain, but it does gives us the chance to see what we need in the midst of it. We must also acknowledge the position of our world and comprehend that when sin entered into it, so did disease and disaster. However, God in his grace also created within man the ability to address the difficult and desperate physical and emotional needs created by the brokenness and pain of the human condition caused by sin in our world. These abilities are embodied in doctors, clinicians, and mental-health professionals, as well as properly educated Christian counselors and pastors.

Clinical Importance: Building the Bridge

As a Licensed Professional Counselor and Trauma Specialist for over 10 years, I have obtained extensive knowledge in the field of mental health. Yet, I still have an abundance of knowledge to gain. Though I have the education and skill, I have also gleaned extensively from those who share their heart cries in a room where they feel safe and heard. Why is it important to validate the clinical role in mental illness? Mental illness has been an overlooked and misunderstood problem in our society for a long time—specifically

overlooked, ignored, and disregarded by the evangelical
community. Yet, we are watching a rise in suicide, in depression,
and in behavioral health diagnoses. It has pushed its way to the
front of our minds as we see our fellow believers, our loved ones,
our pastors, and others battle this type of illness. We tend to treat
them as if they are something to fix as opposed to someone who
needs understanding, empathy, and help. Because of this mindset,
we also tend to give quick prescriptive responses through trite
statements and/or portions of scripture to be applied without
acknowledging that mental struggles may need addressing from a
clinical perspective, not just a spiritual perspective (James 2:16).
Allow me to go back to the imagery of a bridge.

We often take for granted how necessary bridges are to our
everyday lives. How often do you count how many bridges you
cross day-to-day on your way to and from work, or school? Perhaps
you have seen news reports of tropical storms or flash floods
washing away bridges, leaving people stranded on one side or the
other of a river or lake, unable to go in the direction they need to
go to acquire help. Bridges connect roads that allow for individuals
to travel from home to the rest of a culture's infrastructure that
produces the goods and services that humans need to thrive and
survive. If I cannot access employment, or a hospital, or the market
for food and supplies, then eventually my place of residence begins
to suffer and may even need to be vacated.

This scenario describes what we believe to be a real problem for
ministry leaders and Christian counselors, as well as Christians in
need of psychological help with mental health issues. It must be
stated that the Bible possesses an incredible wealth of knowledge
for the health of our bodies, souls, and minds, but it doesn't
explain or address the chemical, physiological, and psychological
issues that may be causing some of the problems we are facing. Its

focus is on God and His redemptive work in human history. In these moments, there must be a strong bridge to mental health resources and interventions that can aid in the processing and application of Biblical truth. This mental health bridge is essential to help connect the mind of a person to the resources necessary to properly apply truth, even the truths of scripture. To ignore biological truths not found directly in scripture is ignoring real-life events in our everyday living like the law of gravity or the creation of electricity. God used these scientific truths to aid in our day-to-day life.

Likewise, we cannot be cut off from the Gospel work of the soul by simply focusing on the psychological and physiological. In the analogy of the bridge, the market and hospital exist to help us live healthy lives in our home community; so our bodies and minds exist to house and aid our spiritual communion with God. We must create a healthy bridge between the applied truths of Scripture through mental and behavioral therapies, and the science of why we are struggling in a certain area to begin with. If my ability for healthy mental processes is inhibited, I will most certainly struggle to process and apply the practical truths of Scripture.

We believe there has been a serious misunderstanding in how psychology, medication, and behavioral health can be used in healthy ways to help people struggling with mental illness both understand the source of their struggles, and apply Scriptural truth to their struggles. When I talk with fellow believers from all denominations about their silent pain, I see a common theme. They are consistently told that there must be something they can do to fix it or, there must be something they are not doing right that is causing it. In some instances, this can be the case, but often this is not the case and speaks to a general lack of understanding, experience, or education. Just as we cannot gain God's unconditional love for us, so we also cannot change the brokenness of this world by simply willing it away. This is why the message of clinical importance is so imperative among the Christian community. We must educate ourselves and our communities on these fundamental truths.

Understanding Mental Illness and the Growing Problem

To accept these truths, it is imperative to first understand that mental illness (depression, anxiety, mood disorders, personality disorders) is an epidemic in our society today. It has always existed, but we are seeing these illnesses metamorphose into deeper issues which are threatening the very thing we hold so dear—life. Mental illness is a part of the darkness that entered our world thousands of years ago, and it has only worsened as time has progressed.

The CDC defines mental health conditions as being characterized by alterations in thinking, mood, or behavior (or some combination of those), associated with distress and/or impaired functioning. Mental health conditions are a result of a variety of factors, including biological and environmental (NAMI.org).

Look at these statistics from the National Institute of Mental Illness that will have most certainly worsened after the fallout from the Covid-19 pandemic. These are the most updated statistics and are based on an annual prevalence rate:

National Alliance for Mental Illness [2]

---

[2] NAMI. (2021, March). *Mental health by the numbers*. NAMI. Retrieved September 26, 2021, from https://nami.org/mhstats.

-      1 in 5 U.S. Adults experience mental illness
-      1 in 25 U.S. Adults experience a serious mental illness
-      17% of youth (16-17) experience a mental health disorder
-      More than 46% of Americans will meet the criteria for a diagnosable mental health condition during their lifespan, and half of those people will develop conditions by the age of 14.

Mental Health America [3]

-      More people are reporting frequent thoughts of suicide and self-harm than have ever been recorded in the MHA Screening program since its launch in 2014.
-      Since the COVID-19 pandemic began to spread rapidly in March 2020, over 178,000 people have reported frequent suicidal ideation. 37 percent of people reported having thoughts of suicide more than half or nearly every day in September 2020.
-      Young people are struggling most with their mental health. The proportion of youth ages 11-17 who accessed screening was 9 percent higher than the average in 2019. Not only are the number of youth searching for help with their mental health increasing, but throughout the COVID-19 pandemic youth ages 11-17 have been more likely than any other age group to score for moderate to severe symptoms of anxiety and depression.

These numbers are increasing rapidly. The statistics recorded are those who sought help and stepped up to acknowledge their experiences. Can you imagine the countless more who would be added if they reached out for help? Living in a fractured world

---

[3] Mental Health America. (2021, March 29). *Mental health and COVID-19: What MHA SCREENING data tells us about the impact of the pandemic*. Mental Health America. Retrieved September 26, 2021, from https://www.mhanational.org/mental-health-and-covid-19-what-mha-screening-data-tells-us-about-impact-pandemic#2020ScreeningDemographics.

produces struggles and suffering. It produces mental illness that so many face and battle for years, and often throughout their entire life. It is vital that we understand this and respond to it as a broken world issue and not just a broken person issue. It is no betrayal to your spirituality to acknowledge your need for help and utilize what God has given to receive it.

Seeking Help: A Biblical and Clinical Perspective

From the beginning of time, God created us for relationships and did not intend for us to be alone (Genesis 2:18, Hebrews 13:5). We are not meant to suffer alone or to go through life alone. We were made for community — with God and with others.

When someone battles mental illness, isolation seems to be the primary emotion or belief in their mind. They think things like "I am alone!" or "No one understands me!". Sometimes they even think "Everyone would be better off without me!" Have you felt these things or know of someone who has? These are common exclamations when the brain is sick and lost. They are also lies from the enemy. Whether or not you can distinguish where it came from or where it began, it's simply not true. We cannot take away the deep-rooted feelings of loneliness, but our Biblical foundation promises us that it is not truth. Somewhere (depending on the root or issue) we began to believe this unwavering emotion of solitude and isolation.

Some of us who experience clinical mental illness struggle to find our way to that truth. Our brains can block us and keep us from finding the foundation of God's promise to be with us and redeem our sufferings for our good and his glory. To be clear, if you struggle with a mental illness, it can be extremely challenging to

122

think clearly and in turn to feel better or differently. Without going into the anatomy of the brain, an easy way to visualize it is like a blockade from one end to another. We can try to will the blockade out of the way, but sometimes we need the right tools to break the blockade down.

One thing is certain: it is dangerous to remain stuck believing these lies and untruths. We must seek help. These emotions, beliefs, and feelings can lead to another road—deeper depression, poor choices, isolation, suicidal thoughts, and death. If we talk about these things more openly, we can demolish what Satan means for evil and overcome it through the tools and resources provided by a holy and omniscient God. This is why at the end of this book we have provided resources to help start the journey towards healing.

Each person is different in the manifestation of what mental illness looks like. One person can struggle with it in different seasons of life due to different factors or circumstances going on. Another can carry chronic depression or another mental struggle for the rest of his or her life. Please read this part out loud: with either, there is hope. These struggles with mental illness are often not without difficulty in the fight, but that's where the goodness of God comes in. He has graciously given resources and continues to grow the field of mental health professionals and educators. Victory in this fight is often only accomplished when someone is willing to admit they need help and reach out for help and support.

Why the Gospel is a Vital Part of the Conversation

It is necessary to reiterate some points where we must have a clear understanding. The Gospel gives us immeasurable hope. When our world was stuck in the chaos of sin and separation from God, he sent us salvation and a chance to be in communion with him again. Hope was given to us the day Jesus took all of our sin and disease (past, present and future) on the cross and gave us a chance at a new life when he rose from the dead. It is this hope that is still very alive in us today. We must always remember that Christ does not promise immediate or automatic healing from every earthly affliction. Through him we do have an eternal life with him, and will see a life with no more pain and suffering once we are gone from this world. Yet, we find throughout Scripture that suffering is a grace by which we are perfected—formed into the perfect likeness of Him who suffered in our place (1 Peter 1:6-7). We are promised that "the sufferings of this present time are not worth comparing with the glory that is to be revealed to us" (Romans 8:18). That is why nothing in this world can heal the way Christ does, and this is at the foundation of who we are.

As I mentioned earlier in the chapter, some of us, as Christians, have adopted the belief that our faith heals us of all suffering. If our faith met a certain measure of God's expectation, then we would be free of suffering. This is simply counter to Biblical truth. It is not that Christ has changed or that the power of God has somehow diminished. The problem is that through the years we have misconstrued the Gospel and the value of suffering. Jesus (through his atonement) gives us freedom from the bondage of sin, but this does not free us from suffering and the sickness of the world.

Having a healthy understanding of these truths allows us to have the mind of Christ through the Holy Spirit that transforms us. We have direct access to the powerful work of Christ in our lives, and through him we have hope. In therapy, there is a foundation that should be interwoven throughout every session and conversation— that is this hope. It is a message that reigns true, that is bigger than man and bigger than any illness, because the Creator of all things provides hope in all things. This has opened my eyes to the fact that I don't choose who I help. The moment I stepped into this field, I gained personal experience into a world I didn't know— into trauma, into real and hidden parts of people's lives—parts that would make me go home and cry at times. I realized I did not possess a super power where I could help everyone and understand everyone. I saw into a world outside of the box of thinking that I grew up in. The mental health field is a calling placed on my life to direct others to the healing power of Jesus Christ. Sometimes that power works differently in each person, but we as humans cannot determine the steps of each human life. God ordains our steps (Prov. 16:9). We can only determine what God has provided during our suffering and sorrow. We will never be fully held back from suffering, but we need to understand that there is hope during our pain, and light in our darkest moments. This, my friends, should give us hope.

A Call to the Church

The topic of mental health has recently begun to be re-evaluated by Christians and churches. Mental illness and brain health should be considered more than just a spiritual issue, but a holistic one— as a disease that requires compassion, education, acknowledgment, and (many times) professional help. The people of God need to turn their hearts, minds, and eyes toward the mentally hurting.

The number of pastors who have taken their own lives has brought attention to the need for addressing the struggles that they and other church leaders are facing. Mental illness is not a new thing. It has been around for a long time. Yet, our awareness of it has continued to develop. Moreover, the problems and heartaches that come from it seem to be at an all-time high in our society today. I am heartbroken to see that mental illness and suicide are so prevalent, especially among our church leadership and our church congregants. I am thankful, however, that this is now being talked about more openly and recognized in Christian circles as being a serious problem. Looking back, I remember watching my dad experience depression after years of serving with little breaks, an abnormal amount of back-to-back funerals he had to preach, and a sadness inside of him that he couldn't figure out on his own. Eventually he sought professional help from a psychologist that attended the church. This psychologist diagnosed him with situational depression and advised him to take a break from ministry and to consider counseling. As a pastor, my dad had to take the difficult step to approach his leadership and share this with them, and ask for time off to help him heal. Thankfully, I saw a church walk alongside my dad as he healed. I saw them acknowledge their pastor's struggle. Even though they didn't understand what he was going through, they understood that their job was to listen, encourage, and to aid in their pastor's healing. There are good stories out there; we simply need to hear about more of them.

It is necessary that we continue to grow, and that growth process must include the body of Christ. The church should be the starting point for healing, not the hiding place from it. As pastors and church leaders, we teach this regularly, but do we exercise it? Often times we believe it for others, but do not practice it ourselves. Growth includes acknowledging that there is a problem, having a healthy understanding of it, being on the front lines ready to talk about it, and creating ministries within our churches to help with it. It also includes partnering with mental health professionals in our communities.

Take a look at these staggering statistics from Lifeway Research:

- 23 percent of pastors acknowledge they have personally struggled with a mental illness.
- 49 percent of pastors say they rarely or never speak to their congregation about mental illness.
- 27 percent of churches have a plan to assist families affected by mental illness.
- 65 percent of churchgoing family members of those with mental illness want their church to talk openly about mental illness.
- 59 percent of those actually suffering from mental illness say the same.
- 53 percent of churchgoers with mental illness say the church has been supportive.
- 76 percent of churchgoers say suicide is a problem that needs to be addressed in their community.
- 32 percent of churchgoers say a close acquaintance or family member has died by suicide.
- 80 percent of pastors say their church is equipped to assist someone who is threatening to take his or her own life.
- 92 percent of pastors say their church is equipped to care for the family that experiences the suicide of a loved one.
- 4 percent of churchgoers who lost a loved one to suicide say church leaders were aware of their loved one's struggles.
- 68 percent of Americans feel they would be welcome in church if they were mentally ill.

- 35 percent of Americans say mental illness could be overcome with Bible study and prayer alone. [4]

Our prayer is that this book will be a resource and a wakeup call. We cannot expect to be spiritually mature without being emotionally mature. We cannot help others without understanding others. As believers and as the universal church we must change our way of thinking and use the sword in battle, and not as a source of protection to keep our traditions. The Bible transforms our lives. It is our foundation for the completing work of the Gospel within us, until the day when we are called home and stand face-to-face with our Creator. Until then, let's grow together by acknowledging that these are real issues felt so deeply by so many hurting people.

---

[4] Lifeway Research. (2018, May 1). *13 stats on mental health and the church*. Lifeway Research. Retrieved September 26, 2021, from https://lifewayresearch.com/2018/05/01/13-stats-on-mental-health-and-the-church/.

Identify Your Struggle

but don't let your struggle become your identity

I (Rob) truly struggled to write this last chapter, even though this was the chapter I most looked forward to writing. I struggled because it would take me months and several books to write everything down that is in my heart to give to you, my fellow fighters reading this open letter. It was easy to tell my story, although it isn't easy to fathom how people's perceptions of me will change as they read some of the details. You would think it would be the easy part to give the hope of the Gospel that I want to give to you now, but as wonderful as the hope of the Gospel is, I find that it is almost too much of a shock to receive sometimes.

I opened this letter talking about the fog of depression. Imagine going from utter darkness into instant sunlight, like coming out of a cave or a dark room directly into unhindered and direct sunshine. Your eyes burn, tear up, and squint to try and adjust. It literally hurts your eyes. The Gospel truth that I want to share now can be a bit uncomfortable and even painful, but without a doubt it will be a blessing as it begins to melt away the ominous heaviness of depression and anxiety. We might even have a tendency to run back and seek refuge in that fog. Certainly there will be days when the fog will return and overtake us, but I trust that the truth I now share will give you the light that will guide you toward hope and help. I have titled this chapter *Identify your struggle, but don't let your struggle become your identity.* This title summarizes the two "take-aways" of the entire letter we have drafted for you. It honestly could be the title for the entire book. I would like to tackle these two truths separately, and then bring them together as a complete thought in closing.

Identifying The Cause of Your Struggles

As it so happens, I am writing these last chapters during the Covid-19 pandemic quarantines. It seems that everyone I speak with is battling some sort of episodic depression or anxiety. Those of us who already battle clinical depression and anxiety are really in the thick of the fog right now. I myself have been struggling with "mask panic", as the lack of oxygen when I'm working in my mask reminds my body of panic attacks in the past, giving me the feeling that I'm wrestling with anxiety again! This has been so difficult for pastors and counselors to navigate because it is hitting every area of our lives. Not only that, it can be difficult to continue talking about deep and difficult struggles when everyone is feeling the same way. Those who might normally have sympathetic ears in listening to you share your struggles are now dealing with struggles of their own and can be less interested in discussing or hearing about what you are currently going through. It is in moments like these that we must remember the ongoing conversation that can and must take place with the abiding Holy Spirit of God.

Perhaps you have been asking God if something is wrong with you, and if you are broken. Maybe you even wonder if you are broken beyond repair. Yes, there is something wrong with you. Yes, you are broken. In fact, you are not alone in this struggle of brokenness. The whole of humanity is a broken species. In reality, it is worse than that, every part of this earth, from species to eco-system to super-structures of oceans and tectonic plates is broken—and it is all broken because of one single moment in history, but not beyond repair and not beyond hope.

God did not create the world to be a place of struggle, a place of depression and anxiety. Genesis chapter 2 gives us a picture of only joy and peace as Adam and Eve walked in the garden with the presence of their Creator. A series of bad choices led to the ultimate undoing of this atmosphere of joy and peace. Adam and Eve chose to see themselves as the source of fulfillment rather than God, and as a result the curse of brokenness has existed ever since. Look at these verses from Genesis 3.

> (14) The LORD God said to the serpent, "Because you have done this, cursed are you above all livestock and above all beasts of the field; on your belly you shall go, and dust you shall eat all the days of your life. (15) I will put enmity between you and the women, and between your offspring and her offspring; he shall bruise your head, and you shall bruise his heel." Genesis 3:14-15 (ESV)

These verses communicate the hard reality of the universal curse of sin, which didn't just break the perfect human condition, but also the perfect condition of the animals as well. The Bible communicates that we are still longing for the ultimate healing from this curse because the world is still broken. Look at this verse from Romans 8.

> "(18) For I consider that the sufferings of this present time are not worth comparing with the glory that is to be revealed to us. (19) For the creation waits with eager longing for the revealing of the sons of God. (20) For the creation was subjected to futility, not willingly, but because of him who subjected it, in hope (21) that the creation itself will be

set free from its bondage to corruption and obtain the freedom of the glory of the children of God. (22) For we know that the whole creation has been groaning together in the pains of childbirth until now. (23) And not only the creation, but we ourselves, who have the first fruits of the Spirit, groan inwardly as we wait eagerly for adoption as sons, the redemption of our bodies. (24) For in this hope we are saved. Now hope that is seen is not hope. For who hopes for what he sees? (25) But if we hope for what we do not see, we wait for it with patience."
Romans 8:18-25 (ESV)

The apostle Paul wrote these verses to the church in Rome. Paul was a person who understood brokenness and pain. We know this because he openly shared that he had a struggle with what he called "a thorn in his flesh" that he admitted he had earnestly asked God to remove from him on three occasions, a request God did not grant (2 Cor. 12:7-9). Paul understood that this struggle forced him to depend on God for strength, and to keep his focus on the ultimate healing that could only be found in Jesus Christ. In this passage in Romans, Paul brings into perspective the hard reality that we are all broken and in need of healing. It is easy to see the brokenness of the world, which is all a result of the fall of Adam and Eve, in things like cancer, or any other disease. It's easy to see the brokenness of sin in war or famine or natural disasters. But what about mental illness? Is mental illness a result of the fall of Adam and Eve, or is it just a result of my unwillingness to be happy and at peace? This question is why I had to collect these letters and write this book! For many reasons, spoken and unspoken, the church is more reluctant to talk about the broken condition of the mind because of the fall of Genesis 3.

I watch the church praise people who battle disease or physical disabilities as brave and faithful for continuing on in the pursuit of the things of God, and rightly so. I watch this same church dismiss people with mental and emotional struggles as people who just need to get their act together and apply scripture to their lives. This flippant and ignorant response is literally causing people to take their own lives in despair. I believe this is because it is very difficult to recognize and qualify mental brokenness.

It is absolutely crucial that we start to see mental illness within the larger theological realm of brokenness caused by Adam's sin. If my body is broken because of Adam's sin (or what theologians call "original sin"), and my mind is housed within my body, then it follows that my mind and emotional faculties have also been affected. When we speak of overcoming mental struggles, we should be clear that we are not speaking about allowing our mental struggles to be the final resting place in our effort to pursue righteousness. Mental illness exists because our minds have been affected by original sin. Mental struggles exist because our minds are ill. The illness, the struggle in itself, is not the sin. In fact, working through and in spite of mental struggles towards loving and serving God and others is one of the most beautiful examples of surrender. It is similar to someone who has a physical handicap choosing to serve God with their bodies in whatever way they can. Let me state it another way: when someone whose mind is broken with thoughts of depression and anxiety, even suicide, still chooses to follow after God through pursuit of spiritual fruit, it is an incredible example of spiritual redemption. This is why we must identify our mental struggles but not let our mental struggles become our identity.

Paul talks about this exact struggle in Romans 7. Listen to this:

> (14) For we know that the law is spiritual, but I am of the flesh, sold under sin. (15) For I do not understand my own actions. For I do not do what I want, but I do the very thing I hate. (16) Now if I do what I do not want, I agree with the law, that it is good. (17) So now it is no longer I who do it, but sin that dwells within me. (18) For I know that nothing good dwells in me, that is, in my flesh. For I have the desire to do what is right, but not the ability to carry it out. (19) For I do not do the good I want, but the evil I do not want is what i keep on doing. (20) Now if I do what I do not want, it is no longer I who do it, but sin that dwells within me. (21) So I find it to be a law that when I want to do right, evil lies close at hand. (22) For I delight in the law of God, in my inner being, (23) but I see in my members another law waging war against the law of my mind and making me captive to the law of sin that dwells in my members. (24) Wretched man that I am! Who will deliver me from this body of death? (25) Thanks be to God through Jesus Christ our Lord! So then, I myself serve the law of God with my mind, but with the flesh I serve the law of sin.
> Romans 8:14-25 (ESV)

You will recall in chapter 5 that I showed from Scripture that the whole human person should be seen in three parts: body, mind, and soul (or spirit). The thinking part of my brain that pivots between my body and my soul can either be taken hostage by a broken body, or be lifted up into a restored and renewed soul or spirit. Romans 8, upon close inspection, shows us exactly how this works. Paul says there is part of him that wants to do evil because of brokenness: his body. He states that there is a new law governing his desires and causing him to want to do good in his spirit (or soul). Between those two points is the mental pivot of the mind, and the mind is where Paul says the battle for sin vs righteousness takes place. So here is the ultimate question in counseling someone with mental illness: if the mind is also affected and broken because of original sin, would not the struggle against the flesh be infinitely more difficult? The answer is a resounding yes! It is much more difficult to put into practice what the spirit wants if my mind, which helps me process what the Holy Spirit is leading my spirit to do, is struggling to properly process spiritual decisions.

In counseling terms: it is difficult to give someone Cognitive Behavioral Therapy if their cognition (mental faculty) is too wrapped up in its own struggles to put into practice the behavioral therapies being prescribed. Therefore, the mind must first be treated and brought into balanced and healthy thought patterns before instruction can be given that will depend on the mind to be put into practice. This is the main issue that churches and believers tend to struggle to recognize when it comes to mental illness and issues like depression and anxiety, not to mention the more oppressive struggles like Bi-polar disorder, Dissociative disorders, Schizophrenia, etc.

As a pastor, my job is to bring the Gospel to light in every counseling session. If every mental struggle is a result of brokenness, and every thing that is broken is a result of Adam's sin (Gen. 3), then we must also be reminded that every healing finds its source in Jesus, who the Bible calls the second Adam (see Rom. 5 and I Cor. 15). The Gospel is the hope of the second Adam, Jesus Christ, who came to meet us and rescue us in our brokenness. If we are going to talk about our struggles, we must always also talk about Jesus meeting us in our struggles through the Holy Spirit, and using our struggles for his sanctifying purposes. It is important to state in this moment that not all our depression and anxiety can be dismissed to Adam's original sin in causation. It is also important to remember that my active sinful decisions are often the cause of my current struggles with depression and anxiety, not just Adam's sin, even though my sin finds its root in Adam's original sin. Sometimes a counselor's best recommended remedy is simply to stop quenching the Holy Spirit (I Thess. 5:19) and do what we know is right. This means that bringing the Gospel to light in counseling the anxious and depressed, even the suicidal, means bringing both the concepts of salvation and sanctification into the counseling discussion.

Don't Let Your Struggle Become Your Identity

The word "Gospel" has become a Christian cliche word with a cliche answer. Personally, I find this somewhat refreshing because I can remember a time a few decades ago when all Christians were talking about was rules and standards. As with all things in Christian culture, words and ideas tend to trend, especially in books, and the Gospel is trending in a wonderful way. The simple and cliche answer to the question "what is the Gospel?" is that it is the good news of who Jesus is and what he has done in paying for and offering us salvation. But that is not where the definition of the Gospel ends, in fact, that is just the beginning!

I grew up hearing preachers treat the Gospel as a message just for an altar call. The Gospel was just the message to get people to surrender to God, and then the message of pleasing God became everything else. Nothing could be farther from the truth. The Gospel is a message of hope for every part of our lives, every second of every day and throughout every struggle we endure. Here is why: When we truly understand the Gospel, we are free to acknowledge our broken human condition as merely a condition, and not our identity!

Here are what I consider to be the most basic 4 tenants of the Gospel. If you are new to the concept of the Gospel, please take time to look up the accompanying passages of Scripture!

1. I am a sinner and deserve death (1 Cor. 15:20-28; Romans 3:23, 6:23).
2. Jesus willingly took my sin and death and offers me his righteousness in exchange (John 3:16; 2 Corinthians 5:16-21).
3. I can be honest about my sin and ask God for forgiveness and rescue (I John 1:5-10).
4. Obedience to the Scriptures brings about the best version of my relationship with God, but I know I will continue to struggle with sin and I can rely on God for help with sin struggles and temptation, and continue to confess my sin because God has already offered me forgiveness (I John 2:1-6).

Tennant number 4 is so important because it reminds us that we are in an ongoing struggle to be like Jesus because of the brokenness of our human condition. Very often, sin happens on the outside because of the mental struggles on the inside due to the brokenness of our minds. Yet, the brokenness of our minds is a result of the sin that has poisoned our DNA going all the way back to Adam and Eve. So, do we sin because of a broken mental condition, or do we have a broken mental condition because of sin? Yes! Both are true. It began with Adam, and it continues in us today.

But the Gospel moves us past this difficult reality into the understanding that we have been made new. We have been given Christ's righteous identity as the passages listed above articulate. We call that identity "positional sanctification". This is a theological term that means I have been set apart from the world and placed on a new path of relationship with God. I have already been accepted. The difficulty is that I am still in a body that is broken and wants to sin because of that brokenness. This means I must work hard, with the Holy Spirit's help, to apply the truths of the Bible so that I can become more like the righteous identity of Jesus outwardly that has already been placed upon me inside my soul. Theologians call this process of learning, growing and changing "progressive sanctification". It means that we are progressively becoming on the outside what God has already recreated us to be on the inside. It is a process that takes our entire lives.

For those us of with depression and anxiety, or any other mental struggle be it situational or chemical, the process can be incredibly discouraging because our mental weaknesses tend to make the battle to become more like Jesus an even more difficult battle to win. Every letter in this book has been collected to help you know that you are not alone in this battle. We, like you, have had to fight the difficult realities of brokenness handed down in our DNA, and work hard not to let that brokenness become our identity. We, like you, have to choose every day to see the goodness of God within the struggle and preach to ourselves the truth that we are not defined by these struggles! We are defined by the righteousness of Christ that rests upon us. God sees us as he sees his own son: perfect! Our mental battles are the stuff of earth, but our identity is the stuff of heaven!

If you hear nothing else from this book, hear this: If your struggle is your identity, you will lose hope. You will give up.

We must begin to see our struggles as part of the design that God has produced in our sanctification process. This means that the very struggles we tend to see as keeping us from becoming more like Jesus, are actually given to help us become more like Jesus!

These perceived weaknesses lead us to the strength of dependence on God.

The Apostle Paul was honest about this very idea in 2 Corinthians 12:1-10 (ESV). See what he says about the weaknesses in his own body:

> "(1) I must go on boasting. Though there is nothing to be gained by it, I will go on to visions and revelations of the Lord. (2) I know a man in Christ who fourteen years ago was caught up to the third heaven—whether in the body or out of the body I do not know, God knows. (3) And I know that this man was caught up into paradise—whether in the body or out of the body I do not know, God knows—(4) and he heard things that cannot be told, which man may not utter. (5) On behalf of this man I will boast, but on my own behalf I will not boast, except of my weaknesses— (6) though if I should wish to boast, I would not be a fool, for I would be speaking the truth; but I refrain from it, so that no one may think more of me than he sees in me or hears from me. (7) So to keep me from becoming conceited because of the surpassing greatness of the revelations; a thorn was given me in the flesh, a messenger of Satan to harass me, to keep me from becoming conceited. (8) Three times I pleaded with the Lord about this, that it should leave me. (9) But he said to me, "My grace is sufficient for you, for my power is made perfect in weakness." Therefore I will boast all the more gladly of my weaknesses, so that the power of Christ may rest upon me. (10) For the sake of Christ, then, I am content with weaknesses, insults, hardships, persecutions, and calamities. For when I am weak, then I am strong."

We don't know what this "thorn" was, although theologians suspect it was some sort of eye problem based on what Paul went through with the blinding light at his time of surrender to the Lord. We do see from the language that Paul really thought God would want to remove it for him to be more effective in his spiritual life, but that was not the case. Paul came to the conclusion that the very weakness he struggled with was to make God's power perfect in his life.

The Apostle Paul also spoke about dealing with stressful suffering as important to building our spiritual character in Christ. Look at these verses from Romans 5:1-5 (ESV).

> "(1) Therefore, since we have been justified by faith, we have peace with God through our Lord Jesus Christ. (2) Through him we have also obtained access by faith into this grace in which we stand, and we rejoice in hope of the glory of God. (3) Not only that, but we rejoice in our sufferings, knowing that suffering produces endurance, (4) and endurance produces character, and character produces hope, (5) and hope does not put us to shame, because God's love has been poured into our hearts through the Holy Spirit who has been given to us."

These verses are very raw and honest with the reality that God really does recognize the need for allowing difficult times into our lives as a part of the work he is doing. This can be hard to accept when we view God as a loving God—and he truly is a loving God. However, we tend to become mistaken in what we interpret as loving. As a parent, coach, teacher, and even pastor I have had to bring disciplines to those I am working with. Some of these disciplines have been in response to a need for correction because of destructive and sinful behaviors. Other disciplines are given to help people be prepared for difficulties they may face in the future. As a dad, I instill rules and chores to teach responsibility and character in preparation for adult life. These rules and chores are a small dose of frustration to prepare and navigate more difficult circumstances later in life. They are character formations. As a soccer coach, I ask my team to run, drill, work out and practice set plays again and again. It can be tiring and annoying, but produces a better result on game day. As a teacher, I ask my students to do research, memorization and material application to be ready for the day when the material will be necessary for life practice. As a pastor, I ask my congregants to take hold of the spiritual disciplines like prayer and scripture memorization not so that the Lord will be pleased (he is not pleased by our righteousness), but so that they will be prepared and armed with sensitivity to the Spirit and the power of the scriptures on days when they need it to stand strong in life. God is our father, a coach through the Holy Spirit, a teacher through his Word, and our pastor. He certainly employs both responsive and preparatory disciplines with us, and often these disciplines come in the form of struggles or trials. We must begin to realize, if we are going to come through these difficult times, that nothing is happening to us that God is not intending to use for our good and his glory.

Paul says there is hope in our suffering that does not put us to shame. This is because God understands that suffering is a real struggle that we are never going to be perfect at navigating. I love how king David stated this idea in Psalm 103 (ESV).

> " (13) As a father shows compassion to his children, so the LORD shows compassion to those who fear him. (14) For he knows our frame; he remembers that we are dust."

Mental struggles are a difficult suffering, but God knows our mental strengths and weaknesses, and he is using both of those parts of our character, along with our physical and mental strengths and weaknesses, to show us how much we need him and how much he can accomplish in and through us, in spite of them.

James, the pastor of the Jerusalem church, stated it this way in James 1:2-4 (ESV):

> "(2) Count it all joy, my brothers, when you meet trials of various kinds, (3) for you know that the testing of your faith produces steadfastness. (4) And let steadfastness have its full effect, that you may be perfect and complete, lacking in nothing."

Counting joy, or seeing the good in my mental struggles does not mean I need to be happy, but it does mean I must seek to find strength from the Holy Spirit, the Scriptures, and fellow believers to help see my situation from a higher point of view. When someone is in a trench of struggle, they tend to suffer from what is often called "trench thought". This means that they can only see down the narrow path of struggle which makes every thought and feeling about that struggle. This can be especially true with depression, anxiety and thoughts of suicide or self-harm. It can be very difficult for a person suffering from trench thought to talk themselves through their own struggles and take hold of the hope that comes with the truth about God's care.

We would recommend that any time someone is battling difficult circumstances that bring about feelings of depression, anxiety, or self-harm that they seek help in the form of a licensed counselor or therapist. Pastors, especially, tend to convince themselves that they can talk themselves through these struggles, but it is imperative that pastors receive wisdom and emotional support outside of their own minds.

As I close this book, let me again say that we are wrapping up this project in the midst of the Covid-19 pandemic. I never dreamed that when we started this project 2 years ago, we would soon enter a time when virtually everyone I know has battled depression in some way within the last 6 months. This has made it even more difficult for those of us who struggled already. Another wave of fog rolls in, a fog that is all too familiar to many of us. My hope and prayer is that in the midst of your latest battle, whenever you may be reading this book, that you will understand the hope found in the Gospel: the good news that reminds us that God is no stranger to our struggles, and that he is actively using them for our good and his glory. Don't seek to see this difficult struggle merely end; ask God what might be strengthened in your faith because of and through this struggle. Ask God how he might use this to sanctify you. Ask God to use this struggle in a way that would be a blessing to others. Ask God to allow your identity to be wrapped up in who Christ is and what he has done for you in giving you his righteousness and taking your sin.

I leave you with this final word of encouragement: you are not alone in your struggles because there are others just like you who are struggling as well, but more importantly, because Jesus himself had to battle thoughts of depression and discouragement. Yes, even Jesus, who already knew the end of his own story, possessing all the knowledge of the Trinity, had some moments of emotional wrestling. Consider these words from the author of the Epistle to the Hebrews in chapter 4 (ESV):

"(14) Since then we have a great high priest who has passed through the heavens, Jesus, the Son of God, let us hold fast our confession. (15) For we do not have a high priest who is unable to sympathize with our weaknesses, but one who in every respect has been tempted as we are, yet without sin. (16) Let us then with confidence draw near to the throne of grace, that we may receive mercy and find grace to help in time of need."

The author of Hebrews wants us to understand that Jesus not only knows about our personal struggles, he can enter them through empathy. He has been there and done that! We cannot take the liberty to say that Jesus struggled with all of our various diagnosed mental struggles. It would be a stretch to say that Jesus was clinically depressed or anxious. We certainly shouldn't go to the lengths of saying Jesus would have been diagnosed as bi-polar or suffering from a personality disorder, but we can definitively state from this verse that he felt the weight of the human condition. This verse tells us he can sympathize (or recognize with understanding) our weaknesses. He faced every human struggle and resisted the temptation to pursue sinful thoughts, actions or reactions. The reason we can say he empathizes, is that the verse goes on to say that we can turn to him for mercy and grace. Sympathy recognizes a struggle, but empathy enters a struggle. Jesus invites us to bring his mercy and grace into our struggle that we might receive help and hope within the struggle itself (vs 16).

This verse brings to mind a couple of instances where the Gospel gives us a glimpse into Jesus' own battle of the mind. The first instance comes to mind from the shortest verse in the Bible: John 11:35 tells us "Jesus wept". What is remarkable about this tiny yet powerful verse is the reality that Jesus, being God the Son, knew he would soon raise his dear friend Lazarus from the dead, yet he

146

still had to battle through the human emotion of grief and loss. More than the theological study of the hypostatic union of Jesus as the God-man, this is a lesson that Jesus was an empath. He felt the human emotion of Lazarus' family, the hopelessness and finality of loss, and it affected him in such a profound way that he wept over a reality that he was soon to change. What this scenario does is speak to our own human condition and the brokenness of this world. We know that heaven will be a perfect reality, undoing all the griefs and struggles that we experience on this earth, yet it is impossible not to feel the weight of emotions and mental wrestling that takes place because of this human condition. This is exactly why we are invited to confidently call on Jesus in Hebrews 4, to come and minister to us with mercy and grace!

Another instance of Jesus wrestling mentally comes to us from Luke 22. In this chapter, Jesus served his last supper to the disciples, and led them out to a garden to pray. It is in this moment we see one of the most "human" moments of Jesus as he says in prayer "Father, if you are willing, remove this cup from me. Nevertheless, not my will, but yours be done" (vs 42, ESV). If there is any doubt that this was a very emotional moment for Jesus, one should simply keep reading on to verse 44 which states "And being in agony he prayed more earnestly; and his sweat became like great drops of blood falling down to the ground"(ESV). This happened right after an angel came to be with him and give him strength. Consider the ramifications: Jesus, being fully God, knowing that he would rise from the dead, and even having the personal ministry of an angel is struggling so much with what he must go through, that his human body is sweating blood. During one of my own bouts with anxiety I suffered a panic attack so sever that I had cold sweats and shortness of breath. It was a physical reaction to emotional struggles that was so severe, I will never forget it. Jesus was in such severe anguish and so intense in prayer that his

human body struggled to process the stress. This moment in Jesus'
life is another example of why Jesus can look at our struggles with
eyes of mercy and grace.

Preaching the Gospel into your trial doesn't mean dismissing or
diminishing it. Jesus did not diminish the trial of his crucifixion,
rather he walked through it knowing it would be hard, and
knowing it would serve a purpose. The Gospel gives us courage to
know pain is never wasted. It leads us forward in God's foot path
of care on Christ's footsteps by the power of the Holy Spirit. My
friend, you are not alone in your struggle. I get it. Krissie gets it.
Others like the ones who have written letters for this project get it.
But none of us matter. Jesus is the one who matters, and he gets it.
He has suffered the brokenness of humanity, but he went on to
defeat the brokenness of humanity. Jesus offers you the freedom
and boldness to bring your struggles out into the light and receive
the soothing balm of his grace and mercy. He offers the grace of
his presence, purposes, and plan for your struggle. He offers the
mercy to forgive your failings within the struggle. Most importantly,
he offers you his never ending love that will carry you forward
beyond the struggle and into the perfection of our future reality in
heaven. This struggle does not have to be the end of your story.
This struggle does not have to be your identity.

Resource Page

The following list is a place to start. We hope and pray that you will not face mental struggles alone, and want to offer a place to start in your quest to receive support, help and hope.

- Krissie has put together a resource page on her website: **krissiejoy.com**.
- **psychologytoday.com**
- Christian Care Connect: **connect.aacc.net**
- Focus on the Family: **focusonthefamily.com**
- **redeemercounselingcenter.com** is based in Orlando Florida but offers telephone and video counseling as well.
- **counseling.redeemer.com** is the link to the counseling ministry out of Redeemer Presbyterian Church in NYC, pastored by Timothy Keller. They offer phone counseling as well.
- **remedylive.com** is a Christian anxiety and suicide prevention chat center.
- **churchandmentalhealth.com** provides suicide prevention resources as well as other resources.
- the national suicide help line is 1-800-273-TALK (8255)

Made in United States
North Haven, CT
10 May 2022

19067069R00090